THE ART OF 11-14S

AGE-RANGE TOOLS FOR LEADING CHURCH-BASED GROUPS

Toolbag Contents

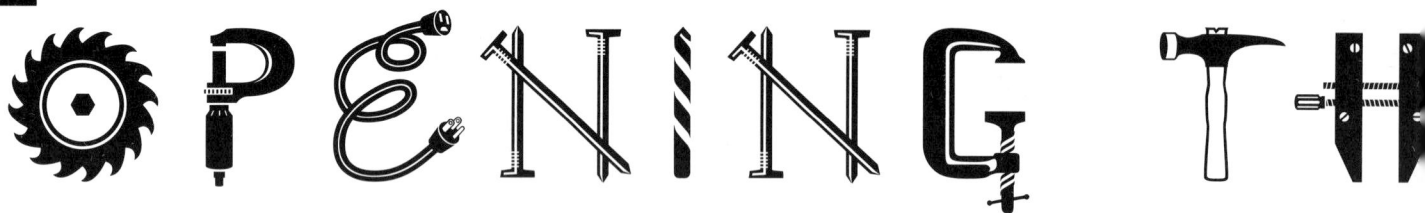

Being a leader of 11 to 14 year olds sounds like hard work – and it is! After all, everyone knows they can be selfish and inconsistent. They worry and disappoint you, and constantly demand entertainment and change. Sometimes it is difficult to know what to do with them – they are definitely not children, yet not exactly teenagers either. They rebel against people thinking of them as 'the children at the top end of the Sunday School', but are often not wildly enthusiastic about taking on the responsibilities that growing up as a vital part of 'the Church of today' demands.

And what about you as a leader? It is not 'hip and cool' to lead a group of 11 to 14 year olds, unlike working with older teenagers. There will probably not be a huge queue of people waiting to join you as leaders. You may often feel taken for granted and unsupported – desperate even.

On top of all this, even the Bible does not say anything explicitly about working with the age group! This is all bad news.

SO WHY BOTHER?

The Bible does, however, have a lot to say about working with 'people', and we can assume that 11 to 14 year olds fall into this category! Everything written in the Bible about spreading the gospel and making disciples is about your group.

The ability of 11 to 14 year olds to respond to the gospel and to be disciples is amazing. They have time on their hands, so most will come to your sessions eagerly. They are not set in their views or ways, and will be prepared to try out new ideas. Many are still vulnerable and will want to share their life with you. They will expect you to share yours with them too. They are beginning to think through for themselves what people tell them, rather than simply accepting it. This is all brilliant news for you as a leader.

And just think – the younger they become Christians the longer they will have to be God's ambassadors and to build up the Church! So in spite of the struggles, you are involved in exciting, strategic work for God's kingdom. That is why you should bother with 11 to 14 year olds.

How the 'toolbag' works

The *Toolbag* series is designed to help you (and other leaders in your church) to explore an issue that is vital to your children's and youth ministry. In this 'toolbag', you will find practical help with running your group of 11 to 14 year olds and with being a confident leader.

You will have the opportunity to

see what the Bible says on the issue, and explore the issue on your own or with other leaders

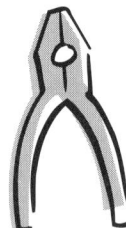

pray about it

get some off-the-peg, practical ideas

make your own notes which will get you into action

hear real-life stories of churches that are working well with 11 to 14 year olds

WOW!

be reminded of what you have learnt in the Wow! boxes.

The right 'tools'

A toolbag has pockets which contain tools – that is obvious – but no toolbag does the work for you... at least we haven't found one yet that does! You will need to rummage through each 'pocket' to find exactly the right 'tool' for the job you have to do. So here are the 'tools' – the rest is up to you, to others in your church, and to God.

Need a hand?

If you are the only leader working with your group, you are still a team – with God! Try to set aside enough time, on a regular basis, to work through the 'toolbag'. Realistically, in order to make room in your schedule, you may have to drop some of your other reading. In any case, keep the 'toolbag' somewhere visible with a Bible and pen, ready to dip into it at any time.

If you do have other leaders in your team, make sure you meet regularly with them. You could use the material in one 'pocket' of this 'toolbag' as the first half of a meeting, with your normal planning and discussion handled much more quickly than usual in the second half.

Timescale

To guide you through the 'toolbag', all the 'pockets' have a timescale attached to them. You need to delve into **Pockets 1** and **2** before you start with your group, **Pockets 3** and **4** during your first six months, and **Pocket 5** nine months after you begin.

If you are already experienced as a leader, you could use this 'toolbag' for your planning and training for a whole year, as a kind of refresher course.

Right now, build into your schedule time to sharpen up your leadership skills with *The ART of 11-14s*, at the appropriate points in the year. Perhaps mark in training sessions on your year planner, for yourself and your other leaders too, if you have them.

On the other hand, the suggested timescale might not fit with your situation. You may be told one week that you will be leading the group the next! In this case, simply use the Index on page 1 to pick out the 'tools' you need at any particular time.

Getting started

Make a date with yourself to dig into **Pocket 1** as soon as you can.

Alternatively, plan a time to get together with your other leaders. Search through the 'pockets' yourself first to select the 'tools' that will be most useful to you all.

We hope you will not only *survive* with your group, but *thrive*. God has plans for your leadership to be good news for you, your group, the Church and, ultimately, the whole world. So go on, think big and enjoy it!

POCKET 1

NOW

You know how it is. You open a book that claims to be really practical, and it starts going on about aims, objectives, strategies, planning and waffly things like that. All you really want to know is how to survive your first group session!

Well, we are sorry to disappoint you yet again. The 'waffle' starts here because the only way to survive your first session and the rest is to keep in mind the big picture of what God wants to do with your group. Then, when they have tied you up and suspended you by the feet from the light fitting, you will be at peace knowing the valuable contribution you are making to the spread of God's kingdom in the world!

Seriously though...

WHAT IS LEADING 11-14S ALL ABOUT?

No doubt you will ask yourself this question after every group session! We find answers in Colossians 1:28-29, as Paul describes his own ministry.

This is our work in a nutshell. Circle the appropriate parts of the Bible verses, and link them by drawing a line to the paragraph that describes them.

It is about Jesus. He is the centre of the gospel, meeting people's greatest need – to be forgiven – and changing their life. So we teach about Jesus and about what it means to follow him. We show how he affects our own daily life. We are living examples of what we teach.

It is about the long term. In fact, it is about eternity. It is not about keeping young teenagers occupied during the service on a Sunday morning, but about giving them the chance to become Christians who last, maturing all the way to heaven.

It is about God's energy. However tough leading the group feels sometimes, God is at work in us, with us and through us. Struggle does not mean he has given up on us.

Colossians 1: 28-29

'We proclaim him [Christ], admonishing and teaching everyone with all wisdom, so that we may present everyone perfect in Christ. To this end I labour, struggling with all his energy, which so powerfully works in me.'

(from *The New International Version*)

It is about everyone. It does not matter how old people are, or if their parents are Christians, or if they have no contact with church at all, or if they come from a rural situation or an urban priority area, or if they enjoy reading or not. God's aim is the same for everyone – he wants as many people as possible to spend eternity with him.

It is about words. 'Proclaiming' (speaking out), 'admonishing' (warning) and 'teaching' (getting to the heart of what the good news of Jesus is all about) mean making sure that what we say is right. The Holy Spirit can use our words to turn young people's lives round completely.

It is about hard work. None of the results are instant – we do not always get to see them. We need to concentrate on the job God has given us to do as leaders – teaching the gospel and building up disciples – and trust him to change lives. We may be privileged to see evidence of God at work in some group members, but we may be very disheartened that some show no signs of change no matter how much we invest in them. We will probably never know how most of them turn out.

In other words...

WOW!c

By leading 11 to 14 year olds, you are doing one of the most important jobs in the world!

II TO I4S – YES!

If you have not done so already, you will soon discover that 11 to 14 year olds are brilliant to work with. Now of course there are exceptions to the rule, but generally speaking they will give you a real buzz – you will feel that you are getting back from them much more than you are giving. The problem with generalizations, of course, is that as soon as you read any description of the age group, you find yourself saying, 'So how come I have a whole crowd of them that are nothing like that? Which planet are these writers living on?' Anyway, it is worth a try.

When 11 to 14s are convinced of the value of the task in hand, they will throw themselves into it with **energy**, **drive** and **enthusiasm**. If they feel patronized, uncomfortable or exposed, they will clam up and simply watch you trying harder and harder to get them interested.

The **questions** they ask are invariably hard. *We* try to get them to answer questions on the level of 'What was white, had wings, appeared in the sky and sang on the night of Jesus' birth?'; *they* come back with 'How do you know angels exist? Have you ever met one? Why does God have them?' Their questions sharpen our own beliefs and faith as we fumble for answers. At the time we are tempted to squirm and go on the defensive; afterwards we are thankful that they have opened a window in our faith that we did not know existed, and more of the light of God floods in.

They can be full of **imagination**, with the right stimulus. If we ask them to write, illustrate, improvize, create artwork, take off-the-wall photos and brainstorm, we shall soon discover ideas and concepts that will take our brain further than we ever thought it would go.

Humour and **fun** are never far away from any learning or social session we enjoy with them. If we do not plan humour and fun, they will invent their own; if we *do* plan them, our group members will be even funnier. If we take ourselves too seriously, we are dead!

However, there is a serious side to 11 to 14 year olds as well. They are often **drawn towards holiness and love** when they see it in others. Quick to spot pretence and hypocrisy, they seem to have an intuitive feel for what is genuine.

With their developing sense of justice comes a **deep compassion** for those who are suffering – perhaps not for those within the group with whom they do not want to show themselves vulnerable, but for those pushed to the fringes of life elsewhere.

Eleven to fourteen year olds are very **willing to be trained** – in fact, usually more willing to be equipped to do a task than to be taught. We have been staggered to discover that some of the jobs and activities that we have kept to ourselves to organize can be done as efficiently and effectively by our group members, and sometimes more so.

They can be a **multi-purpose task force** for getting jobs done. They long to 'do' the gospel, not just hear it. Giving them opportunities, responsibility and gentle guidance often brings out excellent team strength in them. Thinking, planning and organizing are tasks about which they readily say, 'We can do that!'

Above all, the **quality of their friendship** can be amazing. At a time when their own faith may be shakier before it grows stronger, they continue to share the good news by being 'a friend that sticks closer than a brother' (Proverbs 18:24).

Not only do they need Christ and the vital support of the rest of God's people, the Church desperately needs people like them in it if it is to stay vibrant, healthy and creative. We have an incredible amount to learn from them.

AIMS IN BRAINS GO MAINLY DOWN THE DRAIN

Summing up our work in a memorable way is not easy, but a handy one-liner aim will help us, our other leaders (if there are any) and the rest of the church to stay focused on the main point of our work. By yourself or with the rest of your team, try to decide on one. Otherwise, you may get sidetracked or burn yourself out with endless activities that are not really helping you reach your goal.

All the following aims (with one or two exceptions!) are good ones to have, but which, if any, will you adopt as your main focus? Write each on a separate blank postcard.

To show the rest of the church the benefit of having young teenagers as part of it

To discover and experience the truth of the Bible with group members

To give young teenagers a sense of belonging – in Christ and in the church

To keep group members occupied while the adults worship

To build a young teenagers' mini-church within the church

To produce the future adult generation of the church

To equip group members to serve God at home, in our church, at school and in society at large

To encourage personal commitment to Christ and lasting faith in him

To show young teenagers that church and Christians can be fun

To help group members play an active part in the church fellowship

To develop 'whole' young people

To do what the minister wants

(One blank postcard for your own suggestion)

If you are sorting this out on your own, stick the postcards around the walls of your most used room, or on your bedroom ceiling in case you have a sleepless night! Live with them and pray about them until one becomes the clear favourite. If you are hard pressed to choose one, you could allow yourself two, at a pinch!

If you are doing this with other leaders, start by working individually to score the aims in descending order from 12 points (or however many cards you have) to 1 point, starting with your favourite. Add up everyone's scores for each of the possible aims, and see which aim comes out on top. This is not a very scientific method, so discuss your choice afterwards and pray about it in the light of Colossians 1.

A leg to stand on

It is not by accident that many of the possible aims include the word 'church'. Our young people will not be isolated Christians living just on their own or in the group – they will be a vital part of the Church. The Bible describes the Church as a bunch of 'fellow citizens' (Ephesians 2:19-20), 'God's household' (1 Timothy 3:15) and the 'body of Christ' (1 Corinthians 12:27). 'Separate' is not an option. A leg will not stand on its own.

God wants Christians to meet together as a local branch of the Church so that they can help each other and show the world more powerfully what he is like. Our groups are not churches. They are part of local churches which are parts of the worldwide Church. We know it, and our group members need to know it as well.

You're joking!

Unfortunately, many young teenagers feel distinctly uncomfortable with the rest of the church. Belong to it? They wouldn't be seen dead in it! Well, maybe...

To discover why this might be, we should try to understand 11 to 14 year olds better.

UNDERSTANDING 11-14S

'Little Caring'

Outer Fringe Street

Lower Standards

Dear Pathfinder team

I wonder if you could help me. I'm the leader of St Margaret's, Lower Standards Pathfinders, and I have a problem.

The rest of the church has made it quite clear that they don't want Pathfinders around. They have tried to be quite subtle about letting us know. Things like putting up posters on the main church door saying, 'Pathfinders, do you want to live to be fifteen? Well, keep out then!'; changing the times of the services to 5a.m. and 6.30a.m., just in case, and using only the Latin versions; giving us a shed three fields away to meet in with no heat or power in it; never bothering to find out what we're doing; not involving us in any decision they make. You know the kind of thing.

So what's my problem? No, not the rest of the church's attitude – we think that's just great! The further Pathfinders are away from that lot the better – we can do what we like then! No, my problem is, the posters weren't printed on recycled paper and I think they should have been. What should I do?

Yours hopefully

Ann Arky

Being between eleven and fourteen years old and in church may cause discomfort all round. From the young teenagers' point of view, the problem is that the average church often does not allow for who and what they are. Look at the characteristics of the age group on page 8 and you will see what we mean. However, we must not be drawn into a 'separatist' mentality – there is too much to lose.

HAPPY HOUSEHOLDS

If you are on your own, go through each of the characteristics labels on the next page and write at the bottom of each what the church would have to be like or to do to make young people with this characteristic feel they belong. Of course your group members will have to adapt as well.

If you are with a group of leaders, photocopy the labels and cut them up. Deal them round the group face down like a pack of a cards until they have all been distributed. The aim of the game is for players to get rid of all the labels they have in their hand. They do this by turning over their top label, placing it on a central pile, and saying what the church would have to be like or to do to make young people with this characteristic feel they belong. Players have only fifteen seconds to come up with a sensible suggestion. If they fail, they have to pick up their own label from the pile and also the one underneath. Play proceeds with the next person round the circle. Be strict with the timing!

'Don't laugh at youth for his affectations; he is only trying on one face after another to find his own.'

Logan Pearsall Smith

11-14s

Developing into adulthood, within the restrictions imposed by everyone else

Gap between inner and outer maturity, between physical and mental development

Changing attitudes towards the opposite sex

Increase in abstract thinking, with a broadening world-view and an ability to relate one set of ideas to another

Greater independence from their family

Growth of self-knowledge – the ability to look inward

Sense of personal history, where they have come from and where they are going

Greater excitement about relationships with other people

Greater pressure of expectations from relationships with other people

More choosiness about friends

Girls physically and emotionally ahead of boys by up to two years

Onset of puberty and sexual development

Rapid muscle and bone development

Marked variations in complexion, physical attractiveness and skill

Still storing information eagerly and now able to use it increasingly

Powers of reasoning developing

Find it easy to switch concentration from one thing to another

Losing control of emotions at times

Negative feelings running high and suspicion of authority increasing

Moody, inhibited, uncertain, needing security, acceptance and love

Exaggerated idea of capabilities, with a need to succeed

Asking questions like 'Who am I?', 'Who's right?' and 'What's it all about?'

Hating hypocrisy and waffle, and wanting proof of spiritual claims

Quietly thinking through spiritual things, with outward signs often being deceptive

Seeing the need for a personal faith and wanting meaning and purpose

Increasing desire to be approved of by peers

Peer group setting standards of behaviour as well as style trends

Increasing awareness of conflicting standards and attitudes set by society

Increasing awareness of 'them' and 'us', with some feelings of hatred and fear

Levels of commitment differing markedly depending on family backgrounds

Right now you are juggling in your mind the overall aim for your group, what you know about 11 to 14 year olds in general, and what you know about those who will be in your group. Perhaps the sleepless nights have already begun! So...

WHEN IS A GROUP A GROUP?

Probably the nearest thing to a youth group in the Bible is in 1 Samuel 3 – one aged leader with failing eyesight, one group member, and a huge 'church' to meet in! But just look what effect *that* group had on the world.

The essential features of a group are a caring leader who has a close relationship with God, one young person who turns up, a commitment to exploring the Bible together, and a place to meet. Detailed decisions about who, when, where, what and how are yours to make. There are no rules, only guidelines for the kind of group you believe God wants to see in your church.

On your own, or with any other leaders you have, fill in as many of the practical details opposite as you can. If you are new to leading but the group already exists, you may need to make a lengthy phone call to the overall leader at this point. If you are taking over a group as overall leader, contact the previous leader to get a feel of how the group used to be run, though you will probably have some freedom to change things.

Who?

Tick who you believe are the intended members of the group.

☐ Just young teenagers from church families

☐ Largely young teenagers from church families, but with a few who have no previous experience of church or Christian things

☐ An equal mix of young teenagers from church families and those who are not

☐ Largely young teenagers who have no previous experience of church, but with a few from church families

☐ Just young teenagers with no previous experience of church

The goal is the same for all these kinds of groups, but the way you reach it will be different.

What age?

Most young people in the 11 to 14 age group will be in secondary school. They will all be pre-exam. Will you be flexible or strict about the age group you will welcome? Weigh up several factors. Changing church group the same year as starting a new school can be unsettling. If you are strict about the age grouping, it may mean splitting up friends, or including one 11 year old in a group with ten 14 year olds. You may have a middle school system in your area anyway. If you want 14 year olds to move on from your group, is there a group to which they can go?

Circle the maximum and minimum ages of group members.

8 9 10 11 12 13 14 15 16 17 18

☐ This is a hard-and-fast rule.
☐ This is flexible.

Reason that you could give to a young person or parent who claims that the age grouping is 'unfair'

_____

_____

_____

Style and format of sessions

Tick what you plan to do with your group.

☐ Teaching and learning sessions only
☐ Teaching and learning sessions with an add-on social activity
☐ Teaching and learning sessions with social activity on a different day
☐ Largely social activity with an add-on teaching time
☐ Other _____

_____

At what time?

Try to meet when young teenagers are available rather than when they are not! Remember that those who do not come from church families may have their Sundays planned for them. Put a 'T' against the time when you will run your teaching sessions, and an 'S' against the time for your social activity.

☐ ☐ Sunday morning before the service
☐ ☐ Sunday morning during the service
☐ ☐ Sunday morning going into the service first then out to the group
☐ ☐ Sunday afternoon just before the evening service
☐ ☐ Sunday evening after the service
☐ ☐ Another time on Sunday

_____

☐ ☐ Some time on Saturday

_____

☐ ☐ A weekday evening immediately after school

_____

☐ ☐ A weekday evening later on

_____

Also expect group members to turn up any time on your doorstep! They will appreciate the company of an adult with time to listen. It will revolutionize your relationship with them during group sessions.

For how long?

You may not be able to choose, especially if you have to fit in with the length of a service or with another venue booking. It is always better to leave group members wanting more, but do not make the sessions so short that they are not worth the effort of turning up. Many groups find that between forty-five and sixty minutes is best for teaching and learning, whilst ninety minutes seems about right for social activities. Of course the timing of socials will vary if you include outings.

Put a 'T' against the length of time you will normally meet with your group for teaching and learning, and an 'S' against your social activity timing.

- ☐ ☐ 15 minutes
- ☐ ☐ 30 minutes
- ☐ ☐ 45 minutes
- ☐ ☐ 60 minutes
- ☐ ☐ 75 minutes
- ☐ ☐ 90 minutes
- ☐ ☐ 105 minutes
- ☐ ☐ 120 minutes

Other amount of time for learning

_____

Other amount of time for social activities

_____

Where?

As far as possible, keep to the same venue, though try to meet socially in a more 'relaxed' place than for teaching sessions. Choose venues that are easily accessible and not embarrassing to young teenagers who are very conscious of their image. Ideally venues will have enough space for the group to meet all together as well as in small huddles. There should be as few distractions as possible. A group that meets in an amusement arcade may find concentration difficult, but at least one group has met in a pub and another in a greenhouse! What makes any place acceptable is the way leaders treat the young people in it.

Normal venue for teaching and learning

_____

_____

Normal venue for social activities

_____

_____

How many leaders?

One is enough. One of each sex makes good pastoral sense (leaders building up close, supportive relationships with group members of the same sex) and relieves the pressure of always being in the limelight. A ratio of one adult to ten young people is the guideline for school trips. One leader to every car-load of group members is a luxury.

Ideally we would have ☐ leaders for the number of young people.

How many group members?

One young teenager is enough, though for safety, one leader should meet with one group member only in full public view. Two young people and one leader can make a very exciting dynamic, with the possibility of working more as a 'team' than as a 'group'. Small groups often know much more clearly why they are meeting and what they plan to achieve. Group members will feel highly valued, as long as the programme you run is at least as exciting as a larger group's would be.

Larger groups often help young teenagers to remain as anonymous as they want to be and offer the kind of 'buzz' that says 'This is a happening event!' In the end, though, the size of the group is not important as long as what you do together is lively, often demanding, sometimes adventurous, and the relationships between leaders and group members are strong.

Our group would feel right if there were about ☐ young people in it.

Identity

Young teenagers want us to take them seriously as individuals, but they also need to belong. Find a group name that has credibility. Perhaps your group members themselves could invent one – something that would help them explain to their friends what kind of group it is. However, you will need exceptional courage to stick with a name *they* dream up!

Having a name like 'Pathfinders' can be exciting because it relates to a wider network of thousands of young people getting together for the same purposes. However, your group will only get excited about the network if you convey *your* enthusiasm for it convincingly.

Group name _____

_____

Annual budget

Stop! Don't go any further until you know how much your group will cost to run each year and from where the money will come. If your church has very little money, raise your own funds and have fun doing it. Also, giving money is a part of worship that your group members (and you yourself!) might not know about or take seriously enough. Make sure your church council knows how much it costs even if you do not actually ask them for the money.

£........ Hire of venue

£........ Teaching resources

£........ Refreshments

£........ Posters for room decoration

£........ Craft materials, paper and other stationery

£........ Pens and pencils for group members

£........ Photocopying

£........ Stamps

£........ Overhead projector acetates and pens

£........ Leader training

£........ Expenses and gifts for guest speakers

£........ Phone bill

£........ Subsidies for special social activities

£........ Prizes/incentives

£........ Total

Now check out all these group details with your vicar, church leader or youth and children's work co-ordinator, to make sure he or she is happy with what you plan to do.

BEING A LEADER

Maybe you grabbed this 'toolbag' wondering what you are supposed to *do* as a leader. Hopefully you have begun to discover some answers. However, it is just as vital to sort out what you need to *be*.

DO-BE-DO-BE-DO

When Paul wrote to church leaders Timothy and Titus, there were false teachers not just outside the Church, but also within it. They claimed that material things (including people's physical bodies) were bad. So they either cut themselves off from the 'impure' world or lived immorally because what they did with their bodies had no effect on the state of their souls. Myth was mixed with truth.

Today's climate is similar – tolerance towards any philosophy, thought or religion as long as it is tolerant itself. Many believe there is no absolute truth. Choosing their favourite bits from any religion or philosophy, they create their own to match their chosen lifestyle. Essentially, they live as they like. For this kind of situation Paul says that what we *are* is just as important as what we *do*. If the gospel is to make any impression at all, we must be distinctive. Explore 1 Timothy 4:7-16; 5:1-21; Titus 1:6-9; 2:11 to discover what leaders need to be.

Be godly Being godly means our 'speech', 'life', 'love', 'faith' and 'purity' will remind people of God (1 Timothy 4:7,12,16). Our words, the quality of our lives, our attitudes towards others and our commitment to them, our relationship with God and how we view ourselves count most in leadership.

Be learners As leaders we do not have to be perfect, but making progress (1 Timothy 4:7,15; Titus 2:11). As soon as we feel we can take off our 'L' plate, it is time to step down from leadership. We make mistakes. We learn on the job. As we work hard at living obediently to God, he makes us more like himself.

Be Bible teachers We need to teach the Bible (1 Timothy 4:13). In teaching sessions we will do this by lively, creative, action-packed methods, and in social activities by living out the truth of the Bible.

Be pastors 1 Timothy 5:1-21 reveals a pastoral heart. Timothy should care so much for the people that he will know what is going on in their home lives, challenge what they do wrong and

support those in real need. In other words, he will want the very best for them and help them at great cost to himself.

We don't need to be perfect to be leaders, just progressive!

O COME, HOLY SPIRIT

'O come, Holy Spirit, inflame my heart, set it on fire with love. Burn away my self-centredness so that I can love unselfishly. Breathe your life-giving breath into my soul so that I can live freely and joyously, unrestricted by self-consciousness, and may be ready to go wherever you may send me. Come like a gentle breeze and give me your still peace so that I may be quiet and know the wonder of your presence, and help diffuse it in the world. Never let me shut you out; never let me try to limit you to my capacity; act freely in me and through me, never leave me, O Lord and giver of life!'

(from *It's Me, O Lord* by Michael Hollings and Etta Gullick, reprinted by kind permission of Mayhew McCrimmon Ltd).

Caring deeply

One feature of our deep care for young people will be our concern for their safety. If you have not already completed the kind of form you see on page 13, photocopy it, fill it in and hand it to the person to whom you are responsible for your work – the overall leader of the group, your youth co-ordinator or church leader.

CONFIDENTIAL DECLARATION FOR YOUNG PEOPLE'S LEADERS

CONFIDENTIAL

This form is to help you, the youth work organizers, and the parents of the young people attending to have every confidence in the care we shall provide. It is in no way a comment or judgement on your qualities, but will be filled in by all leaders. If you have any questions about it, please direct them to

_____ (name of supervisor)

Guidelines from the Home Office following *The Children Act 1989* advise all voluntary organizations, including churches, to take steps to ensure the safety of children in their care. We would like to take notice of this advice for our young people's groups too. In accordance with the House of Bishops' *Policy on Child Abuse,* you are therefore requested to make the following declaration:

Have you ever been convicted of a criminal offence (including any 'spent convictions' under the *Rehabilitation of Offenders Act 1974*) or been cautioned by the police or bound over to keep the peace? (1)

☐ Yes

☐ No

If 'Yes', please state the nature and date(s) of the offence(s), continuing on a separate sheet of paper if necessary.

Have you ever been held liable by a court for a civil wrong or had an order made against you by a matrimonial or family court?

☐ Yes

☐ No

If 'Yes', please give details, continuing on a separate piece of paper if necessary.

Has your conduct ever caused or been likely to cause harm to a child or put a child at risk, or, to your knowledge, has it ever been alleged that your conduct has resulted in any of these things? (2)

☐ Yes

☐ No

If 'Yes', please give full details, including the date(s) and nature of the conduct, and whether you were dismissed, disciplined, moved to other work or resigned from any paid or voluntary work as a result. Please continue on a separate sheet of paper if necessary.

Signed _____ Date _____

Notes

(1) Because of the nature of the work for which you are applying, this post is exempt from the provision of Section 4(ii) of the *Rehabilitation of Offenders Act 1974,* by virtue of the *Rehabilitation of Offenders Act 1974 (Exemptions) Order* 1975. You are therefore not entitled to withhold information about convictions which for other purposes are 'spent' under the provisions of the Act and, in the event of appointment, any failure to disclose such convictions could result in the withdrawal of approval to work with children or young people in the church.

(2) a: A 'child' for this purpose means anyone under the age of eighteen.

b: 'Harm' includes ill-treatment of any kind (including sexual abuse) or impairment of physical or mental health or development.

c: This question relates to any conduct, whether as a paid employee, a voluntary worker, or otherwise.

THE HIGHEST STANDARDS

The Children Act 1989 only legislates about work with under-eights. However, all work with children and young people should be of the highest possible standard. If we follow the recommendations for our group of 11 to 14 year olds, we shall be doing even better than the law currently requires!

Space

Try to provide enough room for each group member to have 2.3 square metres of *unencumbered* space, that is, with no stacks of chairs or other furniture around.

Toilets

The ideal is one toilet and one handbasin per ten young people. Try to avoid the use of roller towels.

Warmth and cleanliness

Group areas should be warm, adequately lit and ventilated. Maintain high standards of cleanliness.

Food preparation

If you want to prepare food at your venue, the area will have to be checked by the Environmental Health Office (unless it is a home). If group members bring their own sandwiches to any event, ideally they should be refrigerated. Drinks must be available at all times.

Special needs

Be able and willing to accommodate young people with special needs. Be aware of access to your building and toilet facilities.

Health and safety

Always have easy access to a phone. (This could be a mobile phone.)

Adults must be aware of safety and fire procedures. A fire drill should be carried out regularly. Fire extinguishers should be available and regularly checked.

Young teenagers with infectious illnesses must not attend.

Smoking should not be permitted near the areas where group members will operate.

Accidents should be recorded, with a note of any action taken, and each record should be signed by the leader involved. A first aid kit should always be available and its location well known. No medication should be administered without written parental consent. One leader should ideally be a first aider.

Insurance

All groups need public liability insurance against a court awarding compensation for damage and also against someone suing a leader personally, rather than the church. Make sure your church's policy covers all your activities both on and off site. Check it with your church leader, administrator or treasurer.

Administration

Keep an up-to-date register and record of children, their parents (and contact phone numbers), attendance and other specific medical information (such as whether they have asthma, epilepsy, diabetes or allergies). The sample record card on page 15 will give you a shape with which to work.

DESIRABLE STANDARDS

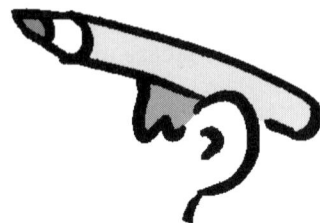

SAMPLE RECORD CARD

(Name of group)1997 Parental Consent Form

Anything written on this form will be held in strictest confidence. In order to be able to meet your child's specific needs, as far as possible, the group leaders need to know these details.

Please return this form to us the next time your child attends (name of group).

I give permission for my child to attend (name of group).

Child's full name _____

Address _____

Home phone number _____

Date of birth _____ Age _____

Name of a friend who attends _____

Phone number where you can contact me in an emergency _____

Name and phone number of GP _____

Details of any known conditions, allergies etc. (e.g. asthma, diabetes) _____

_____

Any other special needs or requirements that it would be helpful for the leaders to know about

_____

In the unlikely event of illness or accident, I give my permission for medical treatment to be administered where deemed necessary by the nominated first aider of the group, or by suitably qualified medical practitioners. Should my child require emergency hospital treatment, I authorize an adult leader to sign on my behalf any written form of consent required by the hospital if I cannot be contacted. However, I understand that every effort will be made to contact me as soon as possible.

I also confirm that the above details are correct to the best of my knowledge.

_____ (Parent/Guardian)

Signature _____

Date _____

ON THE SPOT

Keith Morrison is the leader of a Pathfinder group in Witnesham, Suffolk. He says, 'I started as a Pathfinder leader when I was nineteen – after a long year of discovering that under-elevens weren't for me! I was a member of a church which had a large Pathfinder group. This was a great training ground for me.'

'The most rewarding thing about being a leader is seeing the reality of Christianity sink down deep into the hearts and lives of Pathfinders and, in the long term, meeting them years later as mature Christians. The down side is that I have seen some turn away; either we lose them from Pathfinders or else they drop away from faith afterwards. Sometimes we just have to let go. It's very hard.'

'I lead Pathfinders because I long for young people to know God. I'm desperate for Pathfinders to know what we're on about. It's important work. We may not often know the outcome of it in an individual's life, but we need to trust that the seed that God has planted will grow by the power of the Holy Spirit. It's this trust that keeps me going.'

THE COST OF LEADERSHIP

Being a leader will be hard and painful sometimes. When it is, we can easily lapse into double-speak – saying the 'right' thing but actually meaning something else.

Try to match up what leaders might say with what they actually mean. Join the two with a line. Don't take it too seriously!

What they say

'Leading the group has been a very valuable experience for me.'

'It has been a great challenge for me.'

'The Lord has been teaching me a lot recently.'

'I'm working hard at my relationships with the young people.'

'During last week's session I just handed it all over to God.'

'I've found the insights of other church members really helpful.'

What they mean

'It has been murder and I feel like giving it all up.'

'I hate them!'

'They were totally out of control.'

'I've made some huge mistakes.'

'I'm sick of getting flack from everyone!'

'I'm hopeless!'

Help!

However, you need help, and this help needs to be in place right from the start of your time as a leader. In his book *Restoring Your Spiritual Passion* (Highland 1986), Gordon MacDonald suggests we look for people to have around us who will play six different roles. To finish with this stage of your preparation, invite people (more than one!) to play these roles for you, so that you keep things in perspective and stay sane! Tick the boxes when you have succeeded in finding people who are committed to supporting you in the particular roles.

☐ **Sponsor** Someone to encourage, guide and reassure you that you are on the right road

☐ **Affirmer** Someone to take notice of what you are doing and becoming, and to attach value to it

☐ **Rebuker** Someone to tell you the truth, even though it is mutually painful

☐ **Intercessor** Someone to hold you up to God in prayer

☐ **Partner** Someone to share the load and give you courage and strength

☐ **Pastor** Someone to be there when you are exhausted, to help you make sense of life again

Causes

As rewarding as the work is, leading young people has in-built tensions. Parents and church leaders may have expectations that we consider too high. We shall always be the go-betweens for our group members and the rest of the church. Since young teenagers and their culture are always changing, we shall constantly need to adapt the way we do things. Everyone will be watching our lifestyle. We shall always be questioned and questioning, and sometimes feel very lonely. We shall have to make an extra effort to be 'fed' spiritually ourselves. We have a tremendous responsibility. We need to be constantly creative... Is that enough? Well, maybe just a few more!

Leading young people is emotionally and physically draining. It is usually long-term work, with few 'instant' results. We shall open the floodgates for criticism and misunderstanding. There will always be hard choices to make. We shall often be disappointed by our group members. We shall need to become more and more vulnerable rather than 'stronger'. Now that is enough!

So do you still want to be a leader? Of course you do, because what you are doing will have eternal consequences for the lives of your group members.

POCKET 2

ONE MONTH TO GO

Things are really hotting up now – even more so if there is only one *week* to go! You need to start thinking about your first group session. What will you actually do with them? What will they be like? What do you need to prepare? This 'pocket' will help with planning a programme, teaching and learning, and building relationships with group members – the key elements of your work. There are also some ideas about publicity and more safety guidelines that are vital for protecting both your young people and yourself.

PLANNING A PROGRAMME

The Bible not only contains the vital truth about God that everyone (including young teenagers) needs to know, but also provides the basis for an exciting, varied programme. There are many ways of exploring it – for instance, through whole book studies, current issues and themes. And as you enjoy the Bible with your group members, you will teach them the lasting skill of handling it

for themselves.

Here are some parts of the Bible that you will want to explore:

The good news of Jesus Aim to teach a clear explanation of the gospel once a year, and do not be afraid if it keeps popping up in different ways. In fact, worry if it does not! The whole of the Bible is about the good news of what God did through Jesus, and everyone needs to be reminded of it often.

The Old Testament Not only does the Old Testament contain some gripping stories, but it increases the impact of the New Testament. It tells us who God is, what he is like, and all about his promise and plan for his people. The Old Testament lays the foundations for Jesus' coming. Remember, however, that any principles drawn from the Old Testament should be seen in the light of the New. For example, God's people do not need to sacrifice animals any more because Jesus made the ultimate sacrifice by dying on the cross.

The New Testament In the New Testament we find eye-witness accounts of Jesus' life, his teaching, explanations of what he achieved on the cross, God's idea of what it means to live as a Christian, encouragement to keep going, and the promise of what is to come. Select parts of it to make a series, or study whole books at a time. If you plan to do a series, either

keep it short, or break it up every so often with a one-off, wildly different session.

Issues Your group might be surprised to find out what the Bible has to say on different subjects. On some issues the Bible spells things out clearly in black and white. On others there are grey areas, so it is good to equip your young people to discover the broad scope of what God says about these issues. For ideas, listen for topics raised by your group, the subjects of TV programmes and the news.

Questions Tackle questions that you hear your young people ask, or that they find themselves trying to answer. Struggle together to discover how the Bible answers the questions.

Taboo topics These are the unmentionables in polite company, or perhaps just the unpleasant parts of the Bible or tough things that happen to group members. Include them in your programme to show that Christians recognize them as reality, but more importantly to show what God says about them, rather than letting myths build up out of ignorance.

Themes You could explore different biblical themes and get a grip on what the whole Bible has to say on a subject. Use a concordance to help you find the most useful sets of Bible verses.

Major projects Young teenagers like to be involved in the action and to know they are making a vital contribution. The Bible will shape what you do as a major project and how you do it.

To help you to decide what to include in a term's programme, ask yourself what individual young people need to know about *now*. Keep in touch with leaders of other age groups too so that you know what they cover. For future planning ask your group members what they would like to cover. Give suggestions with tick boxes, and spaces to write down their own ideas. Do not promise anything, but do include some of their suggestions. If you do this well in advance, you can swot up on the subjects about which you do not have a clue, or book people to lead the tricky sessions for you!

Remember, the programme is your servant. You will want to change your plans to meet any special need that arises. But planning in advance does mean that you and your young people will have the security of knowing what is coming up, that you can ask other people to lead sessions for you, and that you can check that you are covering the kind of subjects that will help you fulfil your aim.

PRACTICAL PROGRAMME PLANNING

Either pick up a 'ready-to-use' teaching resource or devise your own scheme from scratch. It is much easier and often more thorough to start with a published resource, even if you decide to adapt what it prescribes. Using material that someone else has created will also give you greater confidence in the early days of leading.

Remember your overall aim for the group. Think how this term's aim might contribute to that. Put it down in a few words.

_____

_____

_____

Which teaching resource will help you fulfil this aim? 'More Tools' on page 48 offers some suggestions to look through in your local Christian bookshop. Alternatively, publishers may be willing to send you a sample copy. Choose a resource that will encourage young people to learn for themselves by being involved, rather than one that simply gives them the answers 'on a plate'.

_____

_____

_____

There will be more help later with constructing individual group sessions and with adapting the published resource to suit your group.

There may not be much time in teaching and learning sessions for one-to-one contact with group members. Brainstorm some attractive social activities. Do not be over-ambitious at first – one or two events a term may be all you can handle. In the future, give your group members a say in what you do.

1 _____

_____

_____

_____

2 _____

_____

_____

_____

PROGRAMME IDEAS ON...

The gospel

• Lead up to Easter using part of one of the Gospels • Lead up to Christmas by looking at why Jesus was born as a human • Give an outline of the gospel that your group members could use with their friends • Go through one of Paul's letters

The Old Testament

• Explore some of the Psalms • Pick out some of the festivals • Shoot through a long book • Linger with a short book • Study different characters • Focus on parts that are quoted in the New Testament • Follow the history of God's people

The New Testament

• Travel through a Gospel • Peruse the parables • Take in the 'I am' sayings in John's Gospel • Spread out a whole letter • Get your minds round the letters to the seven churches in Revelation

Issues

• Self-image • Other religions • War • Parents • Unemployment • Creation versus evolution?

Questions

• Why do Christians think they are the only ones who will go to heaven? • Why aren't there dinosaurs in Genesis? • What about the way the Gospels don't tie up? • How do I know the Bible is true?

Taboo topics

• Sex • Death • Politics • Judgement • Hell • Cliques • Bullying

Themes

• Worship • Sacrifice • Faith • Holiness • God's people, the Church

Major Projects

• Lead a family service together • Write and perform your own Passion Play • Run the crèche at your parish weekend • Care for the homeless

OTHER PROGRAMME IDEAS

PLANNING PUBLICITY

Now how about letting the young people know what you have planned? You need publicity. But who will it be for?

☐ The young people themselves

☐ The whole congregation

☐ The young people's parents

☐ Other _____

_____

_____

Decide what you want to achieve by the publicity.

☐ Getting the young people to the first session

☐ Helping people to pray for the group

☐ Informing parents that something is happening

☐ Other _____

_____

_____

Decide what form your publicity will take.

☐ Sheet given out at the back of church

☐ Newsletter

☐ Programme card

☐ Poster

☐ Display

☐ Advert in church magazine

☐ Local press advert (for reaching unchurched young teenagers)

☐ Other _____

_____

_____

Decide how frequently your publicity will appear.

☐ Once a week

☐ Once a month

☐ Once a term

☐ Once every six months

☐ Once a year

☐ Other _____

_____

_____

Bearing in mind all these considerations, design, copy and distribute your publicity. The clip art below is copyright-free so can be used to create your own design.

Follow up the first wave of publicity with phone calls to any young people you know who have received the publicity. Speak to parents first to reassure them about who you are and what you want, then invite the young people personally. Remember, though, it is not cool to be too pushy!

IT'S HAPPENING

BUILDING RELATIONSHIPS

You can see it all now. They have piled in for your first group session. They stand around catching up on the latest gossip. As a clued-up leader, you know that you should be chatting to them and getting to know them. You spot a small, innocuous-looking bunch over in the corner. You saunter across and strike an informal and welcoming pose. 'Hi, guys! Wasn't Mr Blobby fab last night?'

They look at you as if you are the saddest person in the world, then turn their backs and carry on chatting. You walk away dejected. What went wrong? There are a few rules about building relationships with young teenagers.

Be yourself Do not pretend to be a 'hip and cool' fourteen year old. They will see through it straightaway. You may be worried that they will think you are old and boring unless you dress in the latest fashions and know all the latest 'in' words. If you try it, you will always get it wrong. In fact, young people like having genuine adult friends who behave as adults and treat *them* as adults.

Remember they are really human and friendly A lot of them would actually like someone older to talk to them, and all of them are human – in spite of appearances! They will enjoy finding out that you are human and friendly too, rather than strange and distant.

Check out their culture No, you do not have to know everything about their likes, dislikes, current fads and fashions. They will let you know soon enough, if you listen. But do try to watch some of the programmes they like, listen to some of their music, read their magazines, play their games and get engrossed in their videos. Then at least they will be pleased you are interested in what gets *them* excited and you will have the start-point of a conversation. You may even find you do have something in common after all!

Genuine relationships Allow conversations and relationships to grow at a natural pace. You will have more than five minutes to get to know your group members, so do not pretend to be more 'pally' than you are. It will take time for you to be able to talk about their faith with them. They will be suspicious (and rightly so) if they feel you do not want to be friends with them but actually see them as potential heads to be counted for God's kingdom. In a large group, work hard at getting to know a small number of young people first who will then feel more comfortable about helping you get to know their friends.

It will not always be easy Sometimes group members will act as if they do not want to know you. They may cut you dead or be plain rude. Normally this will say more about *them* than about *you*. Some young teenagers are insecure and find talking to new people even more scary than you do. Their defence is often to be offensive, so that they do not look stupid. Persevere with them. Try to find ways of befriending them that do not rely on much conversation – for example, sharing a bag of crisps or playing football. Often, those who reject you most are actually desperate for your friendship.

WOW! FANTASTIC TO KNOW

Get to know young teenagers better by

trying to understand their world

finding subjects of common interest to talk about, without pretending to know it all

using natural opportunities, like in the car on the way home

persevering carefully

allowing conversations to develop naturally

wanting to talk to them as a friend rather than as a teacher

refusing to see them just as possible converts to Christianity.

BETTER SAFE THAN IN THE PAPERS!

Always have in mind the worst that could possibly happen. Imagine there has been a disaster in your group. You are being blinded by the flashguns of the local press; pushy people are firing questions at you from every side. It is far too late for 'if only'. You know *now* that it was simply not worth taking the risk.

Work through these details with your church's treasurer, administrator or overall leader.

Insurance

Basic insurance for group sessions You must have cover for public liability. This will take care of any compensation that a court may award for injury or damage. Check specifically that your policy holds good with regard to your younger group members as well as the older ones. Ask if you and other leaders or voluntary helpers are covered in the event of parents suing you personally, rather than the church.

Find out from your insurance company what your policy does not include. It may not cover, for instance, travel or any equipment you use infrequently. You can make a special arrangement to have these added to your policy.

'Hazardous activities' may also be outside the scope of the policy. These include not only the obvious activities like mountain walking, but also, perhaps more surprisingly, events like charity walks. You may have to give details of 'hazardous activities' to your insurance company before your group takes part in them.

If you meet on church premises, the church is likely to have insured the building and contents against fire, theft and accidental damage. Do not take it for granted though. Check it out. If you meet on premises that do not belong to the church, find out to what extent you are liable for damage.

If you hire or borrow anything, from a playing field to a camcorder, you may need to get temporary insurance cover for it. Your insurance company may ask to see a copy of the hiring agreement before being willing to give you the required cover.

Insurance for special events You may wish to consider insuring leaders' or group members' personal effects against loss or damage, and to include loss of money and group personal accident.

If you take your group on an outing or holiday, you may have to extend your cover for equipment that is in transit or used in a different location. Decide whether you should also arrange temporary cover for the accommodation in which you are staying and for loss of money.

If you hire a minibus or other vehicle, you will need motor insurance. Include full third-party cover for passengers, other people's vehicles and houses. Remember that your insurance could be invalidated if your driver is not legally permitted to drive the vehicle you are using.

In 'More Tools' on page 48 you will find details of insurance companies and other agencies that offer advice on all aspects of cover for your group, including taking them away on a residential.

Leader accountability

As well as signing the kind of statement that appears on page 13, you and your other leaders should be accountable to your church leader, a church warden, someone on the church council or a well-respected church member. This person should get to know you personally, pop in to see you at work every now and again, and arrange to take up references for anyone who joins you later as a leader.

Work through these details on your own or with your other leaders.

Physical contact

Avoid physical contact with young people as much as possible. This is a very sad thing to have to say, but the current climate of suspicion, and justifiably extreme concern for young people, makes it necessary.

Individuals have grounds for complaint if they describe any physical contact as 'unwelcome'. It is easy for physical contact to be misinterpreted by the individual involved or by an onlooker, and you must always be above reproach. Young people have been known to make false allegations against a leader on purpose, and in these circumstances you should have no shadow of doubt hanging over the way you have behaved with them.

Keeping a healthy distance is actually easier than it sounds. There are few situations in which there is no alternative but to make physical contact. However, if physical contact is absolutely necessary, such as when administering first aid, try to make sure that you are in sight of at least one other adult. If your group is playing a contact sport, volunteer to be the referee or point keeper. If you are enjoying social time together, never let young people sit on your lap.

Do not initiate physical contact, not even a friendly slap on the back, and never use it in response to bad behaviour. The only hard decision comes when young people are upset and look as if they need a hug. Let them initiate the contact, or be sure that it is the kind of contact that they would normally welcome. Perhaps ask their permission, and even then keep the contact very brief. If you consciously choose to make contact, you must be in sight of at least one other adult.

Parent/guardian permission

If you are taking your group out somewhere that is not your normal meeting place, provide a consent form well in advance. Do not let anyone go on the trip who does not bring back a signed form. If you can think ahead to all the kinds of outings you will organize during the year, you may be able to design a form that will do for every occasion and that will only need to be signed once just before the first outing.

The form should enable the person who signs to keep the half with all the details on including times, places, activities and a list of the adults present. Be specific about any activity that is not a normal part of your group session – for example, travelling in an adult leader's car.

On the other half, make sure there is a clear statement of consent for them to sign, with space for them to write down their relationship to the young person, details of where you can get in touch with them during the event and any relevant medical information.

Even though it is very time-consuming to have to chase up pieces of paper, the forms will provide invaluable contact with your group members' homes and you will have confidence in knowing that you are acting thoroughly responsibly.

SAFETY
GUIDELINES
THAT WERE
NEWS TO ME

TEACHING AND LEARNING

'We preach Christ, warning people not to add to the Message. We teach in a spirit of profound common sense so that we bring each person to maturity. To be mature is to be basic. Christ! No more, no less. That's what I'm working so hard at day after day, year after year, doing my best with the energy God so generously gives me.'

Colossians 1:28-29 (from *The Message* by Eugene H Peterson, NavPress 1993)

Maturity in Christ means growing in faith. Faith in him involves belief (thinking), trust (attitude), action (skill) and will (commitment to God). Learning from the Bible grows this all-round faith. When you explore the Bible with your group members, you not only give them knowledge about God, but also help them to change their attitude towards him, and prompt them into actions that please him. Real learning gives knowledge, changes attitudes and offers skills. So how will your young people learn best?

Toys 'R' U

When putting together self-assembly toys, do you –?

☐ **a** carefully read through all the instructions before touching the pieces

☐ **b** assemble them stage by stage, reading the instructions as you go

☐ **c** disregard the instructions and figure out the best method yourself

☐ **d** recall a similar toy you assembled once and work from memory

The answers reveal differences in preferred methods of learning. See if you agree with the following analysis of yourself:

a You are a 'reflective observer'. Watching and reflecting are important for you. You learn well from observation and appreciate having time to make an assessment. You probably enjoy lectures, demonstrations, book reports, listening to good speakers on tape, watching videos – in fact, anything that gives you time to think.

b You are an 'abstract conceptualizer'. Thinking and analysis are important to you. You learn well from rational argument and need a logical presentation. You probably enjoy personal Bible study, character studies, word studies, writing poetry, keeping a diary or journal or listening to expository studies.

c You are into 'active experimentation'. You learn by trying things out and by doing – having a go is important. You need to be involved in practical work. You probably enjoy agree/disagree discussions, field trips, surveys and projects in which you can get involved.

d You prefer 'concrete experience'. Feeling and intuition are important to you. You learn well from past experience and need concrete examples. You probably enjoy spontaneous role-play (as long as it is not called 'role-play'!), and small-group or panel discussions.

You will not be just one type of person when you learn. Most people are a mixture. You might grow to enjoy another type of learning such as, for example, sermons since they are the only learning method on offer during most church services. But, given a choice, you will tend to opt for one type in preference to the others. You probably learn best when your preferred method is being used.

It is the same for young people. So try to use a variety of learning methods, and to teach less but in many different ways. Then all your group members will enjoy learning for at least *some* of the time. However, you yourself need to feel happy with what you are doing. If you are hopeless at giving talks, forget long bits of input. On the other hand, if you are a talented speaker, use your gift. Remember, though, that familiarity with a method is not the only way of gaining confidence. Preparation and experimentation help too. You may surprise yourself and discover new abilities!

PLANNING A LEARNING SESSION

Choose your aim Have an aim that clearly addresses your group members' needs. Ask 'What do they need to know from these Bible verses?', rather than 'What can I do to fill an hour?' Also think 'What attitude might they need to change? What skill could they gain? What good action might these verses prompt them to do?' Even though published resources usually state the aim of each session, ask these questions anyway and try to understand the Bible verses for yourself first.

Decide how you will fulfil your aim The diagram below shows some key elements of a learning session. If you are using a published resource, it will help you decide which activities to use.

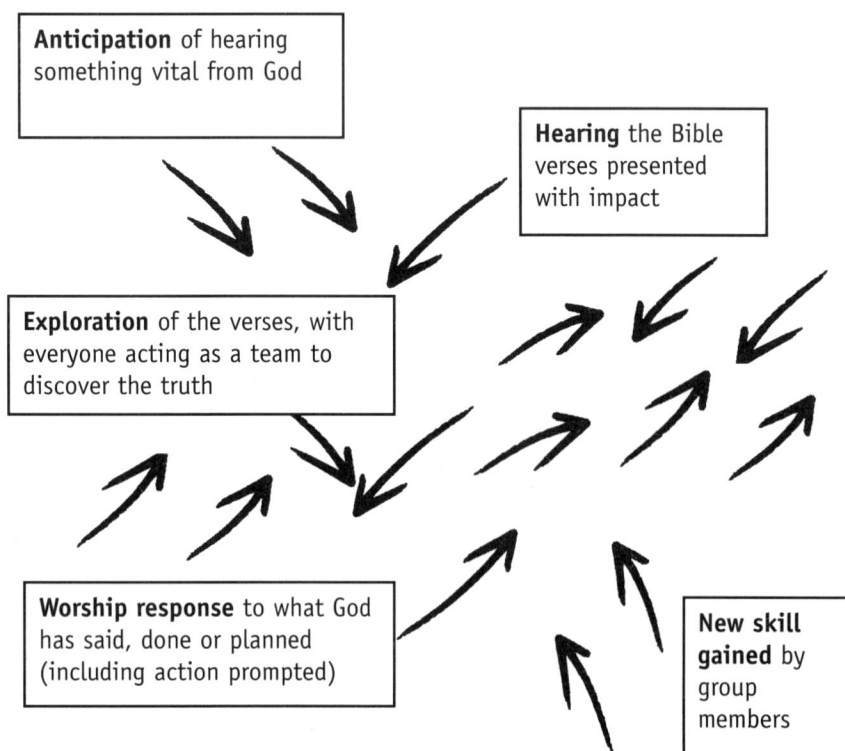

Now choose your activities Bear in mind that people remember what they *do* better than what they simply *hear*, and that activities take up more time than a talk. Involve group members throughout, normally by engaging more than one of their senses. If you are teaching a skill such as meditating on the Bible, do not just talk about it – let everyone have a go.

Adapt the material to suit your group No published resource is tailor-made for your group. After all, you know much more about your group and their needs than the person who wrote the resource. You will always need to change things to suit your young people, yourself and the kind of group you run. Published material will inspire you with ideas rather than provide you with something you can pick up half an hour before a session is due to start.

MAKE IT THEIR OWN

When starting out with a group, it will take quite a long time to adapt the material. The questions below will help you 'make it their own'. Later on, when you get to know your group better and feel more confident about what you are doing, you will be able to do the adaptation much more quickly.

1 Time

The resource may provide a 'supermarket' of ideas from which you have already selected some according to the key elements of a learning session mentioned above. Most of the ideas have a suggested time printed against them. How much time would it take to do *all* the activities you have chosen? How much learning time do you actually have with the group? (Remember to take off five minutes for settling down and five for getting ready to leave.)

2 Ability and Bible knowledge

As it stands, is the material too hard or too easy for your group? Which parts are too hard? Which parts are too easy?

3 Viewpoint

Does your church require a particular standpoint on the issue covered in the material – for example, baptism, or the Holy Spirit?

4 Style

Is your group formal or informal, noisy or quiet? What other adjustment to the material do you need to make, considering what your group members are like and what they can do?

5 Size

Do you need to adapt any of the materials to suit a smaller or larger group than suggested?

Anticipation of hearing something vital from God

Hearing the Bible verses presented with impact

Exploration of the verses, with everyone acting as a team to discover the truth

Worship response to what God has said, done or planned (including action prompted)

New skill gained by group members

6 Age

How mature are your group members? Is the feel of the material too young, too old or just right?

7 Space

Do you have enough space to do the suggested activities?

8 Resources and equipment

Do the suggestions require any resources or equipment that you cannot get hold of?

When you have selected and adapted the suggestions, ask yourself the following questions:

Have I kept to the stated aim?

Is the introduction or first activity gripping enough?

Does the session include hearing the Bible verses, exploring them and time to respond to them?

Is the 'thinking/attitude/skill/will' balance right (page 23)?

Is there enough variety?

Will group members be fully involved in each activity?

Is there anything that will make individual group members feel silly?

Is there still time just to sit and chat with them?

Allocate a realistic amount of time for each part of the session, remembering that the bigger your group the longer everything will take. Also plan your 'escape route'. If one item runs over time, what will you shorten or cut out altogether?

Evaluate the session as soon as possible after it is over What went well? What went wrong? Of which activity should you do more? Find out from your young people what they remember, either by asking them outright or by waiting until they let it out in conversation.

? IDEAS COLLECTION POINT

Make a list of good teaching ideas to which you can constantly add. Here are a few to get you started:

• talk • audio-visual aids like an overhead projector, flip chart or large sheets of paper • group work (vary the size) • ways of sorting everyone into groups • drama • role-play • fish bowl activity (observing a small group in action) • stimulations/simulations • discussion groups • arts and crafts like cut-and-stick, collage- and poster-making • letter-writing • games to 'break the ice', illustrate points, explore the Bible • quiet spaces • skills demonstrations • challenges • problem-solving • summary phrases, limericks or tele-messages (to sum up some Bible verses) • 'Draw the Point' • TV and video • camcorder • photographs • educational games • computers • radio or TV shows (adapted to suit your situation) • slide projectors • debate • story • service • personal illustration • survey • quiz • fun ways of recapping • brainstorms • interviews with friends, group members, church members, in the street or with people who have special jobs • cumulative brainstorm (one idea leading naturally to the next) • cue cards (involvement) • theme evening • reading • bizarre location of meeting • jigsaw • research • paraphrasing of Bible verses • greetings cards • food • scratch-and-sniff Bible exploration • fancy dress on themes • playing • singing praise • testimony • straightforward Bible reading • pass-the-ball discussions (a way of contributing in turns) • humour • funsheets to complete • creative writing

PREPARER'S PRAYER

Lord, as I prepare for our group members, help me to listen carefully to you and to them, so that what we learn together is relevant, makes an impact and changes the lives of all of us.

TOP TIPS ON TEACHING

The creators of the activities in published resources think carefully about making the learning fun and relevant, but here are a few more ideas anyway!

Variety Use a variety of methods to keep interest going (see 'Ideas Collection Point'). Think of a session as a bundle of experiences on a theme rather than as a logical progression of thought.

Visual Make the most of visual imagery, perhaps from the Bible verses or theme. To accompany speech, songs or prayers, use video clips or pictures copied onto overhead projector acetates.

Use a symbol to summarize your teaching. Get group members to practise drawing it so they can take it away as a reminder. They could carry their drawing around in a pocket or bag for the rest of the week.

Bible presentation for impact This should be one of the highlights of the session rather than the 'boring bit'. Help group members to expect to hear from God. Settle them down to be attentive.

Dramatize readings with, for instance, different voices coming from different directions. The *Dramatized Bible* is a valuable resource.

Read the Bible verses with suitable 'mood' music playing in the background or with a picture of the central image displayed for your group to focus their attention on.

Help group members to be involved. Give them something special to listen out for. Or get someone to hold up cue cards (for example, 'Boo!', 'Cheer!', 'Groan!' or 'Smile!') so that the group responds in a particular way to different parts of the Bible verses. Or split them into smaller groups and give each a

character or theme to listen out for and to report back on afterwards.

Ask your group members to stand or do another action every time they hear a particular word or idea.

Turn your room into a map of the part of the world where the Bible reading is taking place. Either have different readers standing in different locations, or move everyone round to follow the action.

Display the Bible reading on an overhead projector acetate with parts of it picked out in colour for the group to join in with reading. Or use colour to show what different characters say and get small groups to read out the different characters.

Always value the immediate reactions of group members to hearing the Bible. What particularly struck, surprised or amused them? If they are self-conscious, they may prefer to write down their thoughts or draw them, or tell them to the person next to them rather than to the whole group.

Slogan Use one or more short, repetitive phrases throughout the session to sum up what you are teaching. Get your group to learn them by heart. Raps work very well.

Story You can tackle almost any topic by telling it as a story. Tell real-life stories from unusual perspectives. For instance, see John 4 through the woman's eyes.

Space The room layout, space and feel can help communicate the theme. For instance, you could black out the room and have special lighting to teach about Jesus being the light of the world, or arrange chairs in a bunch to illustrate that the Church is God's 'family' or in a square to show that it is God's 'temple'.

If possible, run your sessions in places that relate to the Bible verses. For instance, you could go to a tree beside a stream (for Psalm 1), to a hill outside the city, town or village (for Jesus' crucifixion) or to church (for Jesus healing in the synagogue).

Asking the right questions Asking the *wrong* questions can kill a session. Asking the right questions can help you teach your group members, find out what they have learnt and get to know them better. Try:

Open questions, allowing broad expression

'Why are you using this book?'

Useful for encouraging discussion, assessing what group members have learnt and prompting them to apply the Bible personally

Closed questions, limiting the number of possible answers and encouraging 'Yes' and 'No'

'Do you like this kind of book?'

Useful for assessing what group members have learnt or how they have responded, for bringing out the right answers for the benefit of others in the group, and for encouraging contributions

Factual questions, asking for basic information

'How many pages does this book have?'

Useful for bringing out the right answers for the benefit of others and for encouraging contributions

Experience questions, for sharing views and feelings

'How do you usually feel after reading a book like this?'

Useful for helping discussion along, for assessing how much group members have learnt and for prompting them to apply the Bible personally

Rhetorical questions, implying the expected answer

'Won't it be brilliant when you have finished this book?'

Useful for bringing out the right answers, but rather patronizing and manipulative

Leading questions, aimed at getting a specific answer from an individual

'What do you think of this book then, Simon?'

Useful for helping discussion along, for encouraging contributions and for helping group members to apply the Bible personally

Song If your group members are not good at reading, use short songs that can easily be remembered. Do not use books or acetates. You will find some music resources listed on page 48.

Choice of words Help young teenagers to understand and use Christianity's specialist language. They will be happy with abstract concepts like 'faith' and 'mercy' if attached to concrete examples and a brief definition. Later on, 'faith' and 'mercy' will be helpful 'shorthand' ways of expressing a huge amount of truth.

Action For each part of your session, one of the best questions to ask is 'How are the group members active in this bit?' Normally plan to involve more than one of their senses at a time. The following prayer ideas demonstrate that even praying can be physically active.

Prayer Write up one-sentence prayers on a Graffiti Wall, then all step back and pray them silently. For Post-It Prayers, each group member writes a name or prayer phrase on a post-it note and sticks it to the wall.

Postures like standing, kneeling, sitting, looking around and lying flat can help express the mood of prayer.

For a Mexican Prayer Wave, line up the group and give each small section part of a praise phrase to shout in turn as they raise and lower their arms.

Try a Prayer Walk looking, for example, for 'good news' and 'bad news' in the world and bringing it to God.

DISCIPLINE

Then there is always the lurking fear that they will riot! Energetic, fun-loving, confronting young teenagers are normal. The trouble comes when you decide, rightly, not to run your group like school.

Terry Clutterham admits, 'My first major discipline problem came when I was learning to teach. The "lively" class of thirteen year olds were showing no interest in learning. Unable to stand the boredom any longer, one boy dropped his trousers and danced around the room. The class erupted. Well, what would you have done just when you were trying to make a mark in terms of discipline? I'll tell you later how I handled the situation.'

There are some basic guidelines that will help you not to set off on the wrong disciplinary foot with your group. Later on (page 29), we shall do some trouble-shooting. But first the positive approach...

Remember that both you and your group members are made in God's image. You and they should be treated with dignity. Discipline can make young teenagers feel confident about your leadership and secure. Later they may be able to be vulnerable with you and with each other as a result. However, God's image in us is distorted by sin (Romans 3:10-12). Sometimes you and they will get it wrong and will treat each other badly.

Agreed standards With your other leaders, agree on discipline standards, and make them clear to your group. All leaders must always act consistently with the standards, or your young people may play you off against each other. Know exactly what you will do if they overstep the mark. Be ready for challenges to your standards and authority. If you deal with them fairly, they will not last long.

Preparation Work on your teaching material thoroughly. Make sure that everyone will be involved in some way all the time, using their brains, bodies, emotions and creativity.

Equipment Have all equipment set up and working, ready to go without hesitation. Know how everything works.

Room layout Set the room out so that every group member is as close as possible to the leader. Close proximity means better control.

Early arrival Always be in the room before your group members. Claim the territory!

Other leaders If you are running a plenary session, sit leaders in amongst group members, to keep their attention directed on you while you are leading and to discourage messing around.

Relationships Take time to build relationships with individual group members. The best discipline will grow out of respect for you as someone who clearly cares and who invests time and effort in running the group. However, this may take months to achieve. In the meantime, remember that your ministry is essentially about loving the unlovely!

Small groups Spend part of your session time in small groups, according to the number of leaders available. Perhaps even start in groups, if your young people are normally 'high' when they arrive.

Stay calm Never lose your cool. Do not raise your voice in pitch or volume. This reveals panic or loss of self-discipline, and will probably alienate the rest of the group. Instead, practise speaking slowly with a deeper, quieter voice than normal so that you can switch it on when you need to. Pray especially for the 'love' and 'self-control' that the Holy Spirit brings.

'And what about the dropped trousers? The risk was that I would lose all discipline credibility in one minute flat. So I took a deep breath... and laughed along with the rest of the class, saying something like, "Hey, that's really cool! I didn't know you could get boxer shorts that colour!" Then I stood back and watched. Gradually, with the "entertainment" left to run its course, the lad felt more and more silly, and simply sat down. It never happened again, nor anything like it. On the other hand, I'm really glad the headmaster didn't walk by at that moment...'

POCKET 3

THREE MONTHS IN

You have survived – congratulations! However, it would be brilliant if you did more than just survive. How about *thriving* instead? In this 'pocket', you and your other leaders can focus on sorting out discipline problems now that you recognize the danger zones. There are also guidelines on getting to know individual group members and on helping them to grow in God. We start with the bad news!

TROUBLE-SHOOTING

To start off your thinking about discipline (or the lack of it!), try to work out how the following verses help us to think about it – John 13:35, 1 Corinthians 14:33 and Hebrews 12:11.

_____
_____
_____
_____
_____
_____
_____
_____
_____

Now number the following behaviour according to seriousness. Give the least serious a score of 0 and the most serious 14.

☐ Giggling
☐ Eating sweets
☐ Stealing money
☐ Talking while you are talking
☐ Passing notes to their neighbour
☐ Vandalizing a piece of furniture
☐ Fighting
☐ Pinching someone while you are talking
☐ Not joining in the activity you have organized
☐ Swearing
☐ Doodling
☐ Teasing another group member
☐ Being rude to you
☐ Walking around while they should be sitting down listening

☐ _____
_____
_____

☐ _____
_____
_____

Add any other behaviour that you find unacceptable in a group session and give it a score.

With your other leaders, compare your scores. Try to establish a common 'scale of seriousness' list with which you can all work.

Decide together how you will handle each situation if it arises in a session. Plan in terms of both prevention and cure.

Think what behaviour (if any) is bad enough for individuals to be taken back to their parents or asked not to return the following week.

Work out which discipline problems can be dealt with by any leader and which should be referred to one particular leader. Decide who that leader will be.

GROUP DISCIPLINE

EXTRA DISCIPLINARY DOS AND DON'TS

Tick those at which you think you are good, and put a question mark in the box against those at which you need to work harder.

Do

☐ show whenever you can that you are committed to your group members

☐ be well prepared for a session so that you are free to discipline

☐ be natural and relaxed in the presence of group members

☐ make sure that you can have eye contact with everyone in the group from where you are taking the session

OK. SO NOW I CAN SEE YOU!

☐ involve them as much as possible in what is going on, to reduce their time for playing the fool

☐ look for the potential in each group member

☐ focus their attention on what you want them to do, not on what you do *not* want them to do

☐ spread other leaders about the room, rather than letting them sit in a bunch

☐ be consistent

☐ treat your group members how you want to be treated (for instance, do not talk over the top of them when they give feedback)

☐ give clear reasons for rules

☐ use eye contact to control mild misbehaviour, or else use the individual's name in the middle of what you are saying

☐ try to find out *why* a group member is misbehaving before getting too heavy with discipline

☐ be prepared to confront persistent trouble-makers – in the first instance, talk to them privately, appealing to their sense of responsibility to make the group work for each other, spelling out their different options of behaviour and the results of each for the group, and encouraging them to be self-controlled rather than trying to impose control on them

☐ be prepared to remove persistent trouble-makers from the group – if you have other leaders, one of them could escort the group member home; if you are on your own, tell him or her not to return next week, meanwhile contacting parents to let them know what has happened

☐ visit anyone who has been removed from the group, to invite him or her back again

☐ be positive towards individuals whenever you can, especially after you have had to discipline them

Don't

☐ tolerate behaviour that prevents you from meeting your aims

☐ discipline using sarcasm

☐ discipline by making jokes at an individual's expense

☐ take your moods out on your group members

☐ lose your temper

☐ ignore unacceptable behaviour – you can always pick it up with an individual at the end of a session or the beginning of the next one, in a place where you are visible to the rest of the group

☐ be afraid of enlisting parental support

☐ label someone as 'always a trouble-maker'

We think you have the right to know that we nearly called this 'toolbag' *You Can't Beat 11-14s!*

WOW!

HARD TO GIVE, HARD TO TAKE

'No discipline seems pleasant at the time, but painful. Later on, however, it produces a harvest of righteousness and peace for those who have been trained by it.'

Hebrews 12:11

GOOD RELATIONSHIPS

Now we switch to something more positive – how you can build good relationships with individual group members.

I'LL NAME THAT GROUP IN ONE!

Do this activity either on your own or with your other leaders. Get a large sheet of paper and a stop-watch. Give yourself one minute to write down the names of everyone who has been to your group in the past two weeks.

When the minute is up, check the facts with your record of attendance. Has anyone been missed? Has anyone been listed who has been away for the past two weeks? Did anyone come whose face you remember but whose name you forgot?

Go through the list and write one fact about each person beside his or her name. This might be, for example, the name of a best friend or another group or team of which he or she is part.

When you have finished, put the list where everyone can see it. Those people you have named are 'the group'. It is very easy to talk about 'the group' and to forget that it is actually a collection of individuals. Try to get into the habit of conjuring up a mental picture of the individuals whenever you talk about 'the group', to help you keep their needs in mind.

ACTIVE LISTENING

If one of the keys to good discipline is good relationships with your group members, you need to know how to listen to them... *really* listen. Try this listening activity with other leaders.

Split into pairs. For five minutes, one person tells the other something he or she is excited about in leading the group, and something that is causing a sense of struggle. The aim of the activity is for the listener to be able to summarize accurately what the first person has expressed. The two people then swap roles. The following rules hold good for listening to young people in your group too.

Try to listen to each other with undivided attention, even though there are a million things going on around you. Do not interrupt. Keep eye contact, but not so much that it begins to feel awkward for both of you.

Remember what the other person has said, including the details. The harder you listen, the better your memory will become.

Listen to the 'bass line', what the other person is not saying openly but what he or she may be experiencing or feeling.

Watch for non-verbal clues that might tell you how he or she is feeling.

Think about how you yourself might feel in the situation that is being described. It may help you to understand better and begin to empathize with the other person.

Be aware of your own reaction to what the other person is saying. Are you shocked or pleasantly surprised, saddened or overjoyed?

When the conversation is clearly coming to an end, try to summarize in words what you have heard the other person express. Do not repeat it, but paraphrase it. This makes it clear that you have been listening carefully to what has been said.

Building individual relationships with new group members and deepening them with the existing crowd will be hard in a group, but there are ways of doing it.

Allocate pastoral responsibility for each group member to one particular leader, if you are not the only leader. This does not mean that each group member will only relate to one leader, but that no one will be overlooked. If you find that some group members get closer to leaders who do not have

responsibility for them, simply change the listing.

Do activities regularly in the same small groups. In this way, leaders can get to talk to individuals and listen to them more easily.

Offer optional extra groups for those who want to explore the Bible in greater depth. Of course this will cost you in terms of extra time commitment

and more organization, but it will pay back in the long run because of the closer relationships that you will build up.

Run social events. Make sure, though, that you are not chasing around all the time organizing something because you will then have no time to talk to anyone!

ONE TO ONE

What is the use of getting close to individual young people? Draw a line from each statement to the part of the Bible verses that tell us about it. Underline the Bible words or phrases that give you the clues, then pray through the implications for the close relationships you have with group members.

Paul cares for Timothy, with all the responsibility this implies.

Paul encourages Timothy as he faces a difficult task.

Paul has taught Timothy in the past.

Paul challenges Timothy to persevere as a Christian and church leader.

Paul reminds Timothy of the gospel. Remembering the basics is vital.

Paul sets an example for Timothy, especially in suffering for the sake of the gospel.

Paul goes on teaching Timothy. There is always more to learn.

'You then, my son, be strong in the grace that is in Christ Jesus. And the things you have heard me say in the presence of many witnesses entrust to reliable men who will also be qualified to teach others. Endure hardship with us like a good soldier of Christ Jesus. No one serving as a soldier gets involved in civilian affairs — he wants to please his commanding officer. Similarly, if anyone competes as an athlete, he does not receive the victor's crown unless he competes according to the rules. The hardworking farmer should be the first to receive a share of the crops. Reflect on what I am saying, for the Lord will give you insight into all this.

Remember Jesus Christ, raised from the dead, descended from David. This is my gospel, for which I am suffering even to the point of being chained like a criminal. But God's word is not chained. Therefore I endure everything for the sake of the elect, that they too may obtain the salvation that is in Christ Jesus, with eternal glory.

Here is a trustworthy saying:

If we died with him, we will also live with him;
if we endure, we will also reign with him.
If we disown him, he will also disown us.
If we are faithless, he will remain faithful for he cannot disown himself.'

2 Timothy 2:1-13

EVANGELISM OR NURTURE?

Sooner or later (and probably sooner) you will wonder if individual group members are Christians or not. Some may clearly be on God's side; others may make it plain they are not. There will probably be even more about whom you simply will not know. Should you be inviting them to follow Christ or building up a faith in him which they already have?

Growing in secret

Spiritual growth will probably be gradual. Of course *some* will come on in leaps and bounds, but most will not. This does not not mean that nothing important is happening in their lives. Engel's Scale of Spiritual Growth will help you to see that growth can happen which you are in danger of overlooking.

This scale is a theory only, based on observation of what often happens. It is not a blueprint for what *must* happen in a young person's life. Through all your long-term teaching and care, God may nudge your group members along this scale. Sometimes they may slip back. Unless you are careful, you will not even notice. Young teenagers are often too shy to let any personal response show outwardly.

A teaching programme for Christians or non-Christians or a mix need not be very different if it is Bible-based. You will still encourage young teenagers, wherever they are on the scale, to expect to hear from God through the Bible. You will still present the Bible verses for impact. You will still explore it together so that you understand what God is saying. You will still allow space for them to respond to it.

However, there will be a difference in how you might expect them to apply the Bible in their daily lives. In a sense, there is no reason at all why a non-Christian should apply any of it. After all, unless they are committed to God, why should they take notice of what he says? Amazingly, though, some do. On the other hand, you will expect Christian young people to take the Bible seriously, to ask God to change them and to think creatively about how they can put into practice what he says. You will look for them to pray for the fruit and gifts of the Holy Spirit so that they can serve God better with their whole lives. However, equally amazingly, some Christian young teenagers will not do any of these things.

You will have to think carefully then about how you handle the response time in your sessions and about what options you provide for both Christian and non-Christian group members to grow. There are no easy answers, but this is where your individual relationships with them will really count. Make this the main discussion topic and planning need at your next leaders' meeting.

For more help with evangelism and nurture in your group, get a copy of *Groups Without Frontiers* by Terry Clutterham, Penny Frank and Phil Moon, also in the *Toolbag* series (see page 48).

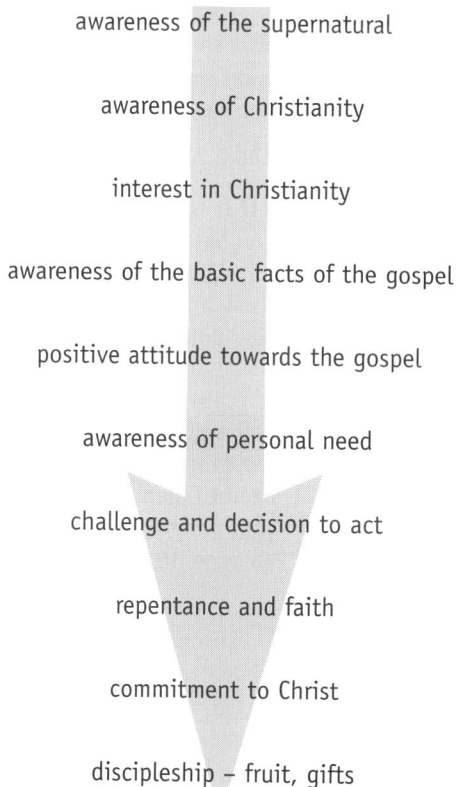

awareness of the supernatural

awareness of Christianity

interest in Christianity

awareness of the basic facts of the gospel

positive attitude towards the gospel

awareness of personal need

challenge and decision to act

repentance and faith

commitment to Christ

discipleship – fruit, gifts

FULNESS

'May the Son of God who is already formed in you, grow in you so that for you he will become immeasurable, and that in you he will become laughter, exultation, the fulness of joy which no one will take from you.'

Isaac of Stella (1165-69)

POCKET 4

SIX MONTHS IN

We hope you are still thinking more about thriving as a leader than just surviving. By this time, you should be feeling more confident about it all – you may even manage to enjoy leadership occasionally!

Strange as it may seem, this is no time to take things easy. This 'pocket' will help you think through the more ambitious leadership tasks of taking your group away on a residential and of keeping in regular touch with their parents. It will also challenge you on the much-closer-to-home issue of how to keep going as a leader.

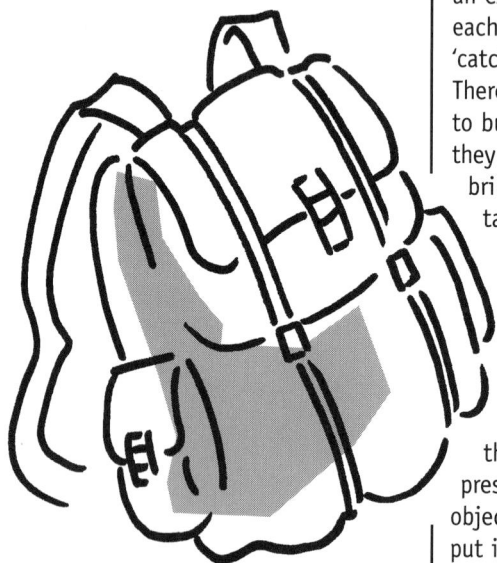

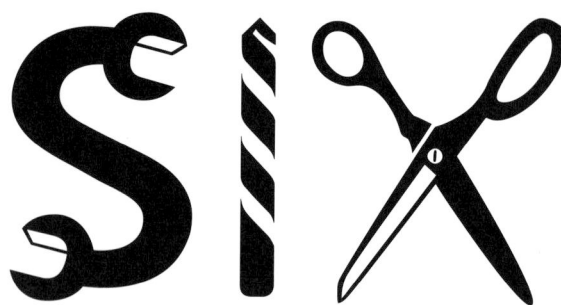

GOING AWAY WITH A GROUP

Residentials are often the highlight of a group's year. With a unique combination of fun, freedom and faith that is hard to beat, they can prove to be very significant times in a young teenager's spiritual life. However, if you still need to be convinced, here are...

Ten good reasons

for going on a residential together

1 It gives you and your group members an excellent opportunity to get to know each other better (warts and all!) and to 'catch' faith in God from each other. There is nothing like a shared experience to build your group together. Whether they actually think the residential is brilliant or rubbish, they will enjoy talking about it for ages afterwards.

2 A change is as good as a rest. It gives extra time to spend with God that you and your young people would not normally have.

3 It gets young people away from their normal life – parents, peers and pressures – so that they can be objective and work out how they can put into practice what they learn.

4 It allows you and your group to do adventurous things you have never done before.

5 It helps your group members to do some quality learning because you can build one teaching session onto another. There is less chance of them forgetting everything between one session and the next. Often they will have the chance to put into practice immediately what they have learnt.

6 It can provide the ideal way for your young people to get together with groups from other churches. Meeting others of their own age with similar beliefs will encourage them and sharpen their faith.

7 It can be a good time to introduce something new into your teaching sessions back home since the weekly rhythm is broken anyway.

8 You and your group members will have a chance to learn about servanthood. There are always plenty of grotty jobs to do on a residential!

9 It shows that Christians can have a good time and that non-Christians do not have a monopoly on fun.

And a final reason just for leaders...

10 It is one of the best training grounds ever. Because of the intensity of a residential there is a steep learning curve and plenty of opportunities to put new skills into practice.

Any well-organized residential will serve the overall aim for your group, so you need to plan at least one a year into your programme. There is help to do this on page 36.

BODY-STRETCHING, FAITH-STRETCHING

Roy Hannell is the Pathfinder leader at St Peter's, Littleover, Derby. He says, 'Without doubt the highlight of our year is our annual weekend visit to Champion House, Edale, in the heart of the Derbyshire Peak District. It's a wonderful opportunity to spend time together, away from the influences of home, parents, brothers, sisters, video and homework.'

'The mix of experiences is vital – working together in teams and having individual responsibilities for domestic chores, for preparing and serving meals, and for clearing up afterwards. Also, of course, we have time to explore a particular Bible theme in many different ways and words. Their participation in the learning stretches their minds to new understandings of just how great and loving a God we have.'

'The seven- or- eight-mile hike we do is a must – only Pathfinders with *two* broken legs are excused! From Champion House in the valley, the long, steep climb seems daunting, but to reach the ridge summit and experience the breath-taking views is a lesson in itself – any valuable achievement, including living to please God, requires hard work, determination and the occasional helping hand.'

'Our group of 11 to 14 year olds sense their own need of direction in life and guidance on the issues that bother them most. They appreciate having boundaries set out in morality and behaviour. They are quick to spot insincerity and double standards, but appreciate being treated as young adults. If within the intense period of a weekend, we can show them love, tolerance and discipline, and be available at all times to talk, they will eventually return this respect and, hopefully, catch another glimpse in us of what God is like.'

PROGRAMME SHAPERS

When planning a residential programme, think

holiday, not school

dreams, not nightmares

unique experiences, not sameness

choice, not uniformity

telling of stories, not talking heads

balance of lasting knowledge, long-term skills and short-term experiences

flexible days, moveable feasts, natural rhythms, the needs of young people

seeing God at work.

AD+VENTURES

Pathfinder residential holiday activities for 11 to 14 year olds are called Ventures, and are run by CYFA/Pathfinder Ventures Limited. Their address is on page 48. Write now for details of spring and summer Ventures to go on with your group. You will never be the same again!

Ad-Venture means

going new places

meeting new people

hearing new stories

enjoying new experiences

daring new activities

learning new truths

applying new discoveries

being new people

shaping new futures.

Scripture Union in Schools also runs an exciting, fun and challenging annual programme of residential events. You will find their address too on page 48.

PLANNING A RESIDENTIAL

Try this countdown. Tick the boxes as you complete each part of the planning.

One year to go

☐ **Date and venue** Decide on your ideal date. Phone schools to find out when their holidays are, if you do not know. Check with the church to avoid conflict with any other major event. Locate a possible venue. For a weekend, make it far enough away to discourage day visitors, but not more than two hours away in all. For a week you could go further. Find out if the venue is available.

☐ **Budget** Plan to cover the cost of the venue, food, transport and any extra activities. Work out what you would ideally like to include in the fee. Compare it with what your young people can realistically afford. If there is a huge difference, try to find other sources of income, or raise money as a group. Do not exclude anyone because of cost. Maybe organize a scheme for paying fees by instalments.

☐ **Speaker** If you want an outside speaker, book one now. You will not need to commit yourself to a topic straightaway, but start discussing the possibilities and then confirm at a later, agreed date.

Nine months to go

☐ **Venue viewing** Never book a venue without seeing it. Check out the site and the people who run it. How flexible are they? Do they like young people and understand their needs? Inspect the bedrooms or dormitories. Take in the

size, shape and number of meeting rooms, the position of power points and any equipment that will be available for sessions and entertainment. Explore the surrounding area. What is on offer? Is there a building, area or piece of local history that could be a feature or theme for the weekend?

☐ **Insurance** With your church leader, administrator or treasurer check what cover you need, particularly temporary cover.

Six months to go

☐ **Transport** If you are going to hire a minibus, sort it out well in advance. Insist on one that has seat-belts. Some counties have their own buses that you can hire relatively cheaply, but your driver may need to take a test. These buses will be very new and well looked-after, compared to other cheap sources. You could hire one commercially, but it will add significantly to your costs. If you plan to ask parents or other drivers from the church, book them now. Let them know when you will confirm if you need them or not.

☐ **Programme** Work out your timetable and the content of the programme before you start to publicize the event. Young people will want to know what they are coming to and what they will be doing in their free time. Parents will be keen to know how much sleep their children will get. (They need a lot!) As soon as you have a topic and a number of sessions, confirm it with your speaker.

☐ **Leaders** By now you will know how many leaders you need. To make it easier and more enjoyable for everyone, do not overload anyone with jobs. The major

tasks will be the cooking, learning sessions and activity times. Give each of these tasks to a different person, and do not give them anything else to do. This could be a good chance to interest other people in leading on a weekly basis. The more leaders you have on your residential the better, without swamping your group members numerically.

☐ **Publicity** Publicize the event. Be really positive. Decide on a campaign so that the way you tell people about it changes each week. Send out information about the programme, along with a consent form and medical form both of which must be signed before a group member can go.

Three months to go

☐ **Discipline** Decide on your rules and how you are going to handle discipline. Refer to pages 28-30 of this 'toolbag'. Spend time together trying to foresee what might happen and how you will prevent it.

You're off!

Make sure everyone knows the expected standards of behaviour and has agreed to them. Check that any who need travel-sickness pills have taken them. Make the departure efficient. If young people are prone to homesickness, they may change their minds about going if you leave them hanging around.

PARENTS AND VISITING

You will be much more effective as a leader if you get to know each group member's parents or other adults at home. These adults make a huge impact on the young people in your group and will help you to understand them much better.

Home visiting

Even with church-going families that you see frequently on Sundays, visiting homes is the best way to build this relationship. It means you are on their territory so they can call the shots. You may also discover another side to the family that you do not see at church!

Think of the adults at home and you as a team. Most of them will be interested to know who is leading the group because they care about their children. Generally speaking, they will appreciate what you do and be supportive of it. They may also be a valuable source of extra help when you need it – it is easier to approach people you know for specific kinds of assistance rather than having to advertize for it in general terms.

However, the support must be mutual. If the adults at home are Christians, your job is to support them in their role as nurturers of faith in their children. They may request your advice about handling particular situations that arise or ask you to tackle a topic in your group sessions that is specially relevant to the family. If they are not Christians, they will still want you to help provide the very best for their children, even if you have different views about what that 'best' might be.

Four excuses for not visiting families at home

1 Get real! I've only just about got time to plan and run the session. Knowing families and understanding your young people may actually mean that you do not waste time putting together inappropriate teaching sessions.

2 I wouldn't know what to say. Go round with a specific purpose, like delivering group programme cards or inviting parents or group members to a special event.

3 It would only embarrass the young people. There certainly is the risk of this, so tell them exactly when and why you plan to drop in. Try to explain why the visit is important. They can then choose to be around at the time or not. Sometimes they find it hard to be in the same room as two adults with whom they behave very differently.

4 I'm not sure what kind of reception I'll get. On your first visit, do not expect to dive straight into a heavy, heart-to-heart conversation followed by extensive prayer ministry! You will probably get no further than the doorstep. Wait for the invitation to go in. Let the family set the pace for the relationship.

HOME VISITING SORTED

Sharing the responsibility

☐ Pray for the motivation to get started on visiting.

☐ Discuss with your other leaders, if you have them, how you can arrange to visit your group members' homes without it being too heavy a burden for you. Try to ensure that the visiting leader is of the same sex as the group member involved and is not too near his or her age.

☐ Stick with the same system of visiting so that individuals are not overlooked.

☐ Put visiting on the agenda of every leaders' meeting you have.

Planning visits

☐ Keep an up-to-date record of attendance that includes dates, birthdays, medical details, addresses and telephone numbers.

☐ Plan to visit the homes of new group members within six months of their arrival. This initial contact visit may take no more than five minutes.

☐ If you are nervous, practise beforehand what you are going to say. As soon as they open the door, be sure to let them know who you are and why you have come. Then enjoy watching the relief on their face when you tell them you are not visiting because their child has been in trouble!

☐ Keep the visit short.

KEEPING GOING

You have been leading the group now for about six months. You are much more confident about the basic job, and are ready to start on other key aspects of the work, like taking your group away on a residential and making good contact with parents. However, you may also feel 'wrung out' and secretly wonder just how you will ever manage to keep going as a leader, let alone become a better one.

HAVE YOU RUN DRY?

Did you know that deserts cover about 20 per cent of the Earth's land surface? That the Atacama Desert in northern Chile is the driest desert on Earth? Parts of it had no rain for 400 years, from 1570-1971, and in other parts, rain has never been recorded. Did you know that the Sahara is expanding southwards at an average of 0.8 kilometres a month? (If not, you should get a copy of *The Usborne Book of Facts and Lists* and make yourself look even brainier than you are!) The desert is a force to be reckoned with. Watch for the tell-tale signs that spiritual 'desert' is creeping into your life. Tick any boxes that you think might describe your current state.

A PHONE CALL TOO FAR

'At the same time as running the church youth group and trying to coordinate all the children's and youth work, I was also organizing a four-day holiday club, burning the midnight oil to "get the show on the road". It was a very ambitious project. The team members had more doubts and fears than confidence and enthusiasm. Every phone call seemed to be more bad news or "tedious" worries.

One evening someone phoned with yet another hesitation about what we were doing – something fairly easily put right. However, it was the final straw. As I put the phone down, I threw myself on the living room carpet and sobbed inconsolably. I astonished myself – it all seemed to have come from nowhere. It was only then that I realized I had taken on too much, deprived myself of too much sleep and, most significantly, neglected my own quality times with God, to enable me to keep things in perspective. Something had to give.'

Terry Clutterham

The good news is that becoming 'better' and thriving rather than just surviving may not mean *giving more*, but *receiving* more. As someone who gives out all the time, you need to receive from God.

As the thirsty wanting water

'We must come to God holding the Scriptures in our hands...

as sinners needing divine pardon,

orphans looking for a heavenly Father,

disciples wanting their teacher,

as a sheep in search of their Shepherd,

as the thirsty wanting water

and as the hungry wanting food,

as seekers after the Truth,

as pilgrims finding the Way

and as the dying wishing to have eternal life.'

(from *Meditating Upon God's Word* by Peter Toon, Darton, Longman & Todd 1988)

Loss of...	Means...
☐ appetite for the work	☐ no dreams for it
☐ energy for the work	☐ no creativity in it
☐ joy and satisfaction in the work	☐ fewer positive thoughts about it
☐ self-discipline	☐ less dependability
☐ time to be *with* God	☐ trying to do more *for* God in your own strength

FLOOD DEFENCES DOWN

Place a glass of clean, fresh water in front of you. Find Isaiah 55:6-13. When God said these words to his people, they were in exile in Babylon, becoming settled, losing the cutting edge of their vision and no longer responding in a lively way to the fact that they were his covenant people and that he was their God. He reminded them that his word – in this case his call to them to repent – was not an added luxury. It was like vital irrigation for parched lands.

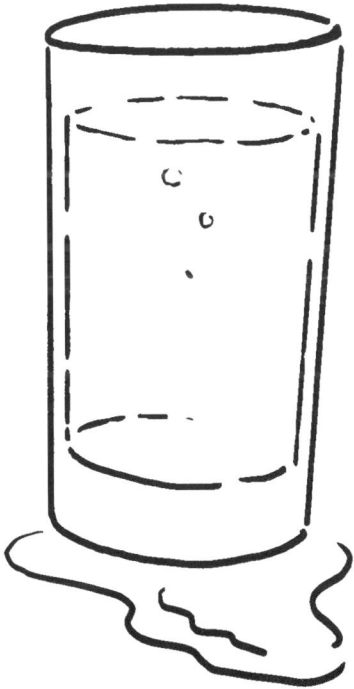

Read the Bible verses slowly and reflectively, sipping and enjoying the water as you do so.

Reflect on what God is saying to you. Imagine the rain and the snow, perhaps especially the snow, so rare in Israel.

Like rain, like snow falling,

Silently, on distant mountains,

Slowly, melting

In due time, in due time.

Streaming from the hills, rushing over pebbles,

Gladly collected, thankfully poured on parched earth,

Refreshing, renewing, transforming the ground,

From the snowy peaks of Lebanon.

Like rain, like snow – my word to you.

Repent. Turn back to me.

And I shall do with you more than you can imagine.

Listen to my word.

My word to you. Trust it.

Repent. Turn back. Be filled with joy.

Consider carefully. We must come to the Bible, to God vulnerably, eager for change, longing for refreshment, flood defences down, ready to be made alive again, as people in desperate need, because that is exactly what we are – in desperate need of intimacy with our Father. Keeping going as a leader begins with a recognition that we cannot keep going in our own strength but are in desperate need of God himself and of his word.

Tell God that this is how you want to come to him, through Bible reading and prayer. If you would find it helpful, cup your hands to pray, as if dipping them into a stream of pure water.

REGAIN GOD'S PERSPECTIVE

1 Build up a thirst for the Bible

Choose the methods of Bible exploration that you think will suit you best, then try some that are not so 'you'. You will find details of many helpful resources in 'More Tools' on page 48.

Reflective, creative approach

☐ Use an imaginative Bible guide.

☐ Try biblical meditation, in conjunction with a study approach. Meditation really means mulling Bible verses over and over again, as in Psalm 119:97.

☐ Combine music, pictures and verses of Scripture (e.g. a psalm). Focus on the words and images that are used, whilst playing some very peaceful music on tape.

☐ Have a go at memorizing short passages of the Bible, so that you can continue to 'chew the cud' on them any time, anywhere.

Practical, hands-on approach

☐ Try down-to-earth Bible reading notes to guide daily living.

☐ Use a paraphrase (like *The Message* by Eugene H Peterson, NavPress 1993) beside your usual Bible version.

Study approach

☐ Ask your clergy for details of home groups that focus on Bible study.

☐ Become a member of a tape library.

☐ Use Bible commentaries. *The Bible Speaks Today* series is especially readable. Find out from your friends which commentaries they have, so that you do not have to spend a lot of money.

☐ Use Bible study notes.

☐ If you are not used to thinking of the Bible as the one big story of salvation, some Bible overview books may take your breath away.

2 Pray

Make your individual times of prayer a top priority. Also, if you meet with other leaders, be 'extravagant' and take exactly half your time together to pray. Your practical planning will not be the worse for it!

3 Keep in mind what you're aiming at

With your other leaders, go back to your aims for your group. Remember, Colossians 1:28-29 will help here. Check all decisions against your aims. Stop doing things that do not help towards your aims.

4 Watch your own relationship with God

Make sure you can be involved in corporate worship somewhere at some time during the week. Focusing on God together with other Christians puts things back into perspective and gives new energy for the job you have to do.

5 Learn to manage your time

Youth work has to be a priority commitment for you. You cannot be a leader, hold six other positions in the church and stay sane for long – unless you are Superhuman! There are five areas of your life which need to be covered by your priority list: personal relationships (including family commitments); personal survival and growth; recreation/social activities; work; church activities.

Across these five, have only seven priority activities, with at least one in each life area. Keep the list somewhere visible. Question anything outside of these seven. If you find your life is too empty, allow yourself another priority activity; if too full, cut one out.

6 Get to know your young people

Sometimes do less 'programme' and have more 'chat'. Learn to enjoy the company of your young people. Receive energy from them. Take them away on a residential break for quality time together.

7 Maintain your support network

Flick back to page 16 to remind yourself of the six people roles to aim to have in your support network. Could you have some of them round for a meal and to pray for you? Do they need more information to help them keep going with their support?

8 Ask for regular training

Book into at least one residential training event and one day course every year. Write or phone for details to the addresses in 'More Tools' on page 48. You change, the children's and young people's scene changes – learning is never finished!

9 Take time off

The work is exhausting, especially if you are leading on your own. Running your sessions during school terms works well, and helps you to know when your time off is coming. Do not feel that your work will suffer if you and your group members have a break. It is preferable to have shorter terms, if necessary, than to organize a rota system for leaders. Your young people need to know you are there for them. With a rota system it is hard to convince them that you are interested in building up a real, long-term relationship with them.

POCKET 5

NINE MONTHS IN

Nine months is a long time to have been leading a group. Leaders usually become experienced pretty quickly! So, with a good grasp of the basics, you may now feel ready to tackle some of the bigger issues like worshipping with 11 to 14 year olds, helping them to participate in the church, and finding new leaders.

WORSHIP

'My group won't sing!' If you have ever screamed this in desperation when asked 'How does your group get on with worship?', you are totally normal! Eleven to fourteen year olds are not renowned for their enthusiastic, tuneful renditions of... well, of anything really! However, praising God in song is just one small part of what the Bible means by true worship.

God calls people to spend their whole lives in worship of him, 'to offer your bodies as living sacrifices, holy and pleasing to God – which is your spiritual worship' (Romans 12:1b). Because he calls our group members to this kind of life too, the time we spend with them must have ambitious goals.

A whole life lived in response to God

The English word 'worship' translates a whole series of Greek and Hebrew words that describe our response to God. These vary from 'bowing', 'kneeling', 'bending' and 'bringing an offering', through to 'serving', 'revering', 'respecting' and 'obeying' – a range of attitudes, physical positions, actions and ways of living that are all obedient responses to the commands God has given to his people. Worship involves

engaging with God in praise and thanksgiving (Ephesians 5:19-20), in personal repentance and holiness of life (John 4)

engaging with other Christians to encourage and build them up in the life of the Church (Ephesians 4:12-13), and

engaging with the world as we tell the good news of what God has said and done (1 Peter 2:9), and as we try to uphold his standards in it (Isaiah 1:16-17; 1 Peter 2:11-12).

Worshipping God with all that we are means keeping this four-way relationship between God, ourselves, other Christians and the world in good order, until Jesus returns. Our worship will culminate in heaven when we see God face to face and know him as he originally intended.

The corporate worship we enjoy with our group is only one small aspect of the worship which we hope will encompass their whole lives. However, during our learning sessions with them, we can offer them a valuable training ground in all aspects of worship. This will involve

prayer

thanksgiving

praise

confession

serving the Church and wider community

celebrating 'festivals'

sacrifice.

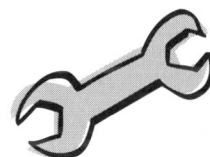

WHERE'S THE WORSHIP THEN?

On page 42 there is a teaching session outline – not necessarily a perfect one! Check out the Bible verses first. Then mark any activity that might encourage your young people to respond to God in worship both during the session and after it. Scribble against different parts of the outline which aspect of worship they might help them develop. Given a wider understanding of what worship involves, what would you like to add to this session to improve it? You may even be able to use this session with your group one day!

HEAVEN

This session should take about **50 minutes**.

Aim of session

To help group members to catch a glimpse of heaven, to begin to grasp what a brilliant place it will be and to live more boldly for God as a result.

Key Bible verses

1 Thessalonians 3:11-13; Revelation 21:1-4

1 Icebreaker (10 minutes)

Set out the room as untidily as possible – chairs upside down, rubbish all over the floor etc. Challenge the group to tidy it up in just ten minutes. Offer incentives, if you are desperate!

2 Anticipation (10 minutes)

Using a graffiti wall (a large sheet of paper stuck up), get group members to write on it things they think are hurtful and wrong in people and in the world. All stand in front of it to pray. Invite everyone to listen to what God says about all the things they have written up.

3 Presentation (3 minutes)

With everyone huddled together as close as possible, a leader recites Revelation 21:1-4 by heart, accompanied by appropriate background music.

4 Immediate reaction (2 minutes)

Ask group members what they pictured in their minds as the verses were being read, and how they felt about it.

5 Exploration (10 minutes)

Everything will be perfect in heaven, including God's people. Sit everyone on the floor around a large, hand-written version of all the Bible verses. Tell the story about the people for whom 1 Thessalonians and Revelation were originally written and what was happening to them at the time.

Get your group to use thick felt markers to underline in green where God will live, ring in purple what God will do, and put an orange box round the things that will not exist in heaven.

All together, go and tear the graffiti wall to shreds – and clear up the mess!

6 Time to talk (10 minutes)

Not only do you want your room to be tidy – you want it to be spotless and perfect! What else can you do to it to improve it? Together make it as perfect as possible, chatting about heaven as you do.

7 Response (5 minutes)

Hear Revelation 21:1-4 again. Guide a silent response.

CORPORATE WORSHIP IDEAS

These ideas come from *DIY Worship* in *The Pathfinder Series* of teaching resources, published by CPAS. *DIY Worship* contains ten themed Bible starters on different aspects of worship, 200 tried-and-tested corporate worship ideas, eleven quality music tracks, worship visuals to photocopy, and Microsoft computer software on CD. There are more worship resource suggestions on page 48.

To get group members praying for each other

Paper Darts

Ask each group member to write down on an A4 sheet of paper their name and what they would like prayer for. When they have finished get them to make the sheet into a paper dart. (You may have to show them how!) Now everyone should hold their dart, stand round the edge of the room, then throw them towards the group members opposite. Tell them to pick up the first dart that comes their way. When everyone has someone else's dart, either get them to pray in pairs straight away, or ask them to take the dart away and pray for that person during the week.

To help group members visualize their confession

Sticky Cross

Psalms 32, 51 • 1 John 1:5-2:2

You will need a cutout of a cross or a wooden one large enough to stick things on. Hand out to your group members stickers that are large enough to write their name on. When everyone has written their name on the sticker, say some words about confession to God, or a suitable prayer. Ask everyone who wants to confess something to come up in silence and put their sticker to the

cross. This will be a sign that they want to accept what Jesus did for them on the cross. At the end say a suitable prayer.

To help young people continue to worship during the week

Wish You Were Here

Hebrews 10:25

You will need envelopes, pens, and postcards or writing paper. Towards the end of a session ask your group members to write a letter or postcard to remind themselves what they have learnt about God. Then they should put down one thing they intend to do in worship of God as a result of what they have learnt. Ask them also to write their name and address on the envelope, pop their letter or postcard into it and seal it. Collect up the envelopes. Tell the group you will send them to their letter or postcard to them later in the week to nudge their memory. Don't forget to post them!

A fun way of helping your whole group to praise God

Hallelujah Mexicana

Psalms 47, 63, 148-50 • Ephesians 1:1-14 • Hebrews 13:15

Gather your group into a semi-circle. If you have a large group they will need to be several rows deep. Explain that the word 'hallelujah' means 'Praise the Lord'. Split the group into four sections. The first section says the syllable 'Ha', the second follow with 'le', the third 'lu' and the fourth 'jah'. Do this faster and faster until the word 'Hal-le-lu-jah' goes smoothly round the semi-circle. Now accompany

this with a Mexican wave. Each section raises their arms as they say their syllable. They bring them down as soon as the next section speaks. See how fast they can go whilst praising God!

A way of using a popular craft activity to worship God

Best of Friends

Find enough embroidery thread for your group members to make friendship bracelets. Brainstorm facts about God, like he made us, he loves us and he helps us. Decide together which you think are the six most important facts. Now ask the group to agree on a colour which best fits each fact about God. It might be red to show that he died for us, blue to show that he helps us, or green to show that he created us. Now make friendship bracelets together using any of the colours you have agreed.

When you have finished, invite everyone to say which colours they have chosen and why. These bracelets might also help group members to share something of their faith with others.

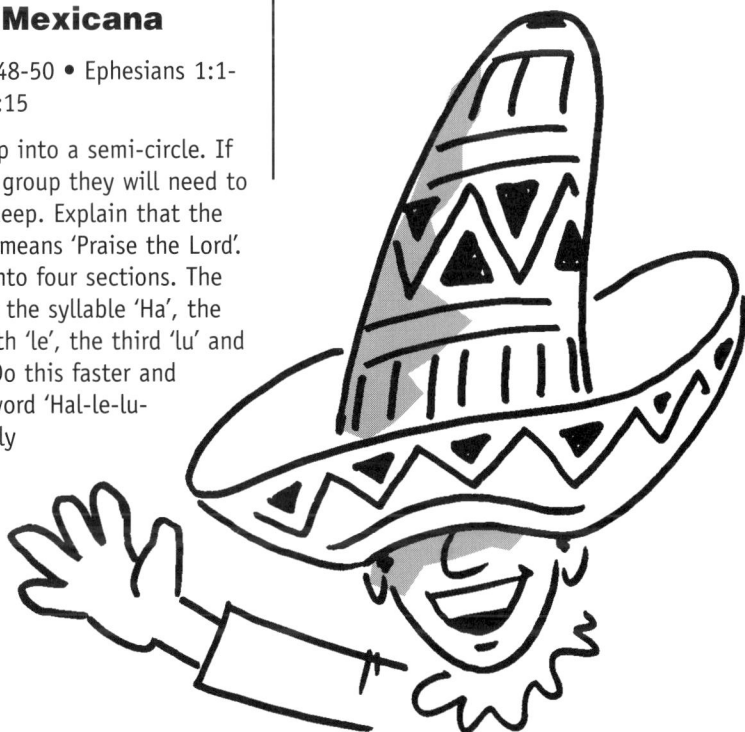

11-14S IN THE CHURCH

This need not be a contradiction in terms! Young teenagers have much to teach the rest of the church and much to learn from it. Enabling this to happen will never be easy though. Essentially, the church wants young people to 'fit' in it; the last thing young people want to do is to 'fit'! It is not part of their 'culture', but we must not give up on the struggle.

Part of their worship of God will involve them in getting stuck in and being servants in a way that counts for the good of everyone. A key question to ask is 'How much can we involve them in?' rather than 'What should we keep them out of?'

Participation

It is not enough to 'cater for' young people – in the end, they will find this patronizing, however good the programme and facilities. They must participate, and 'participation' will mean more than simply getting them used to the way things are. A church's genuine attempt at the integration of young people will involve change for all. Things will be different and better because they are part of it.

We should allow them to contribute 'spiritually' for the good of all when God is clearly at work in their life. Asking them to set out the chairs or make the orange squash is important, but God may just want to say something through them to the rest of the church or involve them, for example, in prayer ministry or sharing testimonies.

However, 11 to 14 year olds are not adults. It is no good asking them to do all the jobs around the church that adults might normally do. For instance, meeting and greeting people at the church door may be death to young teenagers if they are desperately self-conscious. Many of them will not have the self-confidence and 'presence' to lead a service in a way that helps the congregation to feel at ease. Generally speaking, they will assume responsibility more boldly as a group rather than as individuals.

Youth A Part

Youth A Part: Young People and the Church was a report published by the General Synod of the Church of England in 1996. You should be able to order it through your local Christian book shop. It took the broad definition of 'youth' as 11 to 25 year olds, so some of its recommendations are relevant to 11 to 14 year olds, some are not. However, you will find it helpful for setting out the principles for the active participation of young people in church.

IN AN IDEAL WORLD

With your other leaders, first remind yourselves of the good news about 11 to 14 year olds as shown on pages 5 and 8. Now be idealistic. Create the following features of church life to be exactly suited to the age group:

an act of corporate worship

a way of making church decisions

a church social activity

a way of learning leadership within their own church group

informal contact with other age groups

a different way of serving the church.

Now, real life cannot be centred around 11-14 year olds alone, neither should it be. There must be give and take. Having created the ideal world for young teenagers, try modifying your ideas so that you keep the essence of what you have planned, but so that they will be good events for both older and younger people too.

FINDING AND STARTING NEW LEADERS

If you are leading the group on your own, sooner or later you will feel under pressure. Perhaps you already do. Find someone to help you. This person could sort out practicalities like transport, arranging the room, keeping the records, organizing equipment and refreshments, distributing pens and paper, and being around to chat with the young people. However, you will also need someone who will eventually be able to take over from you as overall leader. It is no good waiting until your last day before you start looking around for someone!

If it is not up to you to select new leaders, work through pages 45 and 46 with the person who is responsible for it. It will help him or her to know the kind of person you have in mind. Agree on a course of action by ticking the parts of the plan below that you think you should carry through. Make changes and alterations as you pray and discuss together.

PLAN OF ACTION

Get people praying

☐ **1** Establish a prayer network for your work (see page 46).

☐ **2** Invite any keen pray-ers to observe your group first-hand. Try to break down the barrier of fear of the unknown. Maybe a pray-er will become a leader.

Have a clear idea of who you're looking for

☐ **3** Draw up a job description for the specific leadership task.

☐ **4** Debunk the myths about who can and who cannot be a leader of 11 to 14 year olds (see page 46).

☐ **5** Grasp the principles of who might make a leader (see page 46).

☐ **6** Look around imaginatively and prayerfully at who might be a leader. Try not to have to advertize.

Ensure an ongoing process of support and training

☐ **7** Arrange a good start for him or her by gentle introduction into the scene.

☐ **8** Make sure that someone will take on the role of ongoing review and support for the new leader.

☐ **9** Look for training opportunities from which the new leader might benefit (see page 48).

Prayer network

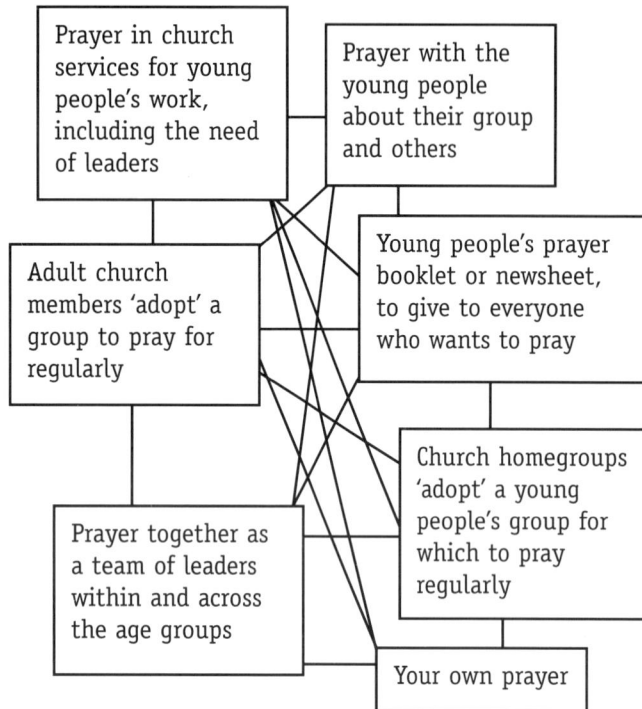

```
┌─────────────────────┐        ┌──────────────────┐
│ Prayer in church    │        │ Prayer with the  │
│ services for young  │        │ young people     │
│ people's work,      │        │ about their group│
│ including the need  │        │ and others       │
│ of leaders          │        │                  │
└─────────────────────┘        └──────────────────┘

┌─────────────────────┐        ┌──────────────────┐
│ Adult church        │        │ Young people's   │
│ members 'adopt' a   │        │ prayer booklet   │
│ group to pray for   │        │ or newsheet,     │
│ regularly           │        │ to give to       │
│                     │        │ everyone who     │
│                     │        │ wants to pray    │
└─────────────────────┘        └──────────────────┘

                               ┌──────────────────┐
┌─────────────────────┐        │ Church homegroups│
│ Prayer together as  │        │ 'adopt' a young  │
│ a team of leaders   │        │ people's group   │
│ within and across   │        │ for which to pray│
│ the age groups      │        │ regularly        │
│                     │        └──────────────────┘
└─────────────────────┘
                    ┌──────────────────┐
                    │ Your own prayer  │
                    └──────────────────┘
```

Debunk the myths

What *not* to believe or say if you want new leaders

1 Young people come from another planet. Being a leader is a pretty gruesome business.

2 Leading young people's groups is not as important as leading adult groups.

3 Only qualified teachers need apply.

4 Up-front teaching is the only job to do in a group.

5 Young people's leaders must be under thirty years old.

6 Leader rotas are good news for the young people and for their leaders.

7 Leaders have to be heavily into young people's culture.

8 It's only for an hour on a Sunday (or a Friday, or ...).

9 Once a leader, always a leader. There's no guilt-free way out.

10 Don't worry about your motives – all young people's leaders are ego-trippers anyway!

Identikit leader?

Remember

None of us was ideal when someone asked *us* to lead for the first time, and none of us is now! But watch for signs of these things happening or starting to happen in the life of anyone you approach to help.

Commitment to Christ

☐ A mature, committed Christian who has known the risen, living Christ for some time

The Bible

☐ Committed to exploring and learning from the Bible, to being changed by it and to living by it

☐ Enthusiastic to help young people to explore the Bible in ways that respect both the young people and also the Bible itself

The Church

☐ Member of the local church

☐ No other major commitment in it

☐ Recognizes young people as a contributing part of the body of Christ – willing to appreciate their culture

☐ Aware of own need to be trained and taught – to grow

☐ Essentially a team player

Signs of Christlikeness

☐ Godly

☐ Reliable

☐ Loyal

☐ Cooperative – submits to leadership

☐ Persistent – emotionally resilient

☐ Enjoys being with young people – loves them

☐ 'An infinite capacity for disappointment' – willing to be vulnerable

☐ Ready to spend time building up relationships with young people and their families

☐ Open to change

☐ Good model for young people to follow

☐ If married, aware of the need to spend enough time with his or her own family

☐ If single, aware of the need to enjoy a social life and close friendships outside immediate church contacts

☐ Able to give enough time to prayer, preparation, meeting with other leaders, and to have contact with young people and their families

☐ Able to give an hour a week to the group learning session, and time for group social activities

Worship

☐ Prayerful

☐ Positive, thankful living

☐ Responsive to God's word and to God at work in people's lives

Names of potential leaders

_____

_____

_____

_____

JESUS AT THEIR AGE

He had vanished. He was not up front of the travelling crowd with the mothers and children, and he was not at the back with the fathers and young men. Jesus simply was not there. Panic!

No doubt Mary and Joseph both imagined he was with the other. Maybe one thought of him still as a child, the other as a young man. Jesus was twelve, ready to become a full member of the synagogue – the Jewish church. From now on, he would be a 'son of the Law'. He would have to learn (and keep) the Law for the rest of his life. But at this moment, for Mary and Joseph, Jesus was their lost little boy.

Meanwhile Jesus was back in the Temple in Jerusalem. He had chosen not to stick with his family – he had wanted to be independent. There he sat, talking with the wise old teachers – asking questions, answering questions and raising issues. When he spoke, you could have heard a pin drop. How could a lad

of twelve ask such searching questions and understand all *this*?

In burst Mary and Joseph, and there followed the kind of 'negotiation' that young people have with their parents every day, when there is a whole lot of not-really-understanding going on and when people get upset. 'Why have you done this to us, son? Your father and I have been worried sick!' 'Well, why were you searching for me? You must have *known* where I'd be – here in my Father's house!'

There was an uneasy pause. Something was not being understood. Something had changed. Some*one* had changed. Probably someone was being hurt. Parents find it hard when their children answer their questions with other questions.

In the brief conversation three things at least became clear (Luke 2:48-49).

Jesus knew who he really was. 'Didn't you know I had to be in *my Father's* house?' But this was the Temple of the Almighty Creator, Saviour and Sustainer God! 'Yes, that's my Father!' was behind what Jesus was saying. More than just a 'son of the Law', he was the Son of God.

Jesus knew where he really belonged. 'Didn't you know I had to be *in my Father's house?*' For Jesus' family, Nazareth had no doubt been full of close, happy days and peaceful nights. Now Jesus seemed to be saying, 'Nazareth is no longer enough.' At this moment, the Temple was somehow closer to heaven – to his real home – than the little house and carpenter's shop in Nazareth.

Jesus knew what he had to do. 'Didn't you know I *had* to be in my Father's house?' Since he realized who he was and where he really belonged, he knew he had to live to please the Father. Being in the Temple meant wanting to serve God – to worship him, learn about him and give back to him. That was why people went there. 'Don't you realize that I simply *must* do what God wants me to do and the time for me to do it is right now?'

'Jesus grew in wisdom and stature, and in favour with God and men.'

Luke 2:52

One of the best jobs In the world

You can do nothing more valuable than help young people to become children of God and to know for sure that they are. You can do nothing more imaginative than encourage them constantly to think of heaven as their real home. You can do nothing more creative than support them as they live boldly for God until they get there. The benefits of most jobs are much shorter-lived than eternity!

MORE TOOLS

USEFUL ADDRESSES

Publicity and tracts
Christian Publicity
Organization, Garcia Estate,
Canterbury Road, Worthing,
West Sussex, BN13 1BW
Tel: 01903 264556

Bible tape libraries
St Helen's, Bishopsgate,
St Helen's Vestry,
Great Helen's Street,
London EC3A 6AT

Anchor Recordings, 72 The
Street, Kennington, Ashford,
Kent TN24 9HS

Training courses for group leaders
Youth and Children Division,
CPAS, Athena Drive, Tachbrook
Park, Warwick CV34 6NG
Tel: 01926 334242

Help with group insurance
Youth Clubs UK, 11 St Bride
Street, London EC4A 4AS
Tel: 0171 3532366
For cheap insurance to
affiliated youth organizations

The Ecclesiastical Insurance
Group, Beaufort House,
Brunswick Road,
Gloucester GL1 1JZ
Tel: 01452 528533
For 'youth combined policies'
as well as ordinary church
policies

Advice Development Team,
National Council for Voluntary
Organizations, Regent's Wharf,
8 All Saints Street,
London N1 9RL
Tel: 0171 7136161
For details about insurance
protection for voluntary
organizations

Association of British Insurers,
51 Gresham Street,
London EC2V 7HQ
Tel: 0171 6003333
For information about which
companies offer specific risks

**Help with residentials,
including insurance**
CCI (UK), PO Box 169,
Coventry CV1 4PW
Tel: 01203 559099

Holiday activities
CYFA/Pathfinder Ventures Ltd,
CPAS, Athena Drive,
Tachbrook Park,
Warwick CV34 6NG
Tel: 01926 334242

Scripture Union in Schools,
207-209 Queensway,
Bletchley, Milton Keynes,
Buckinghamshire MK2 2EB
Tel: 01908 856000

RESOURCES

CPAS Code	Title	Author and Publisher
	HOW-TO RESOURCES FOR LEADERS	
03591	Christian Youth Work	Mark Ashton, Phil Moon, Monarch
03622	The Church and Youth Ministry	Pete Ward, Lynx
03648Y	The Adventure Begins	Terry Clutterham, CPAS/Scripture Union
C18001Y	Groups Without Frontiers	Terry Clutterham, Penny Frank, Phil Moon, CPAS
	Youth A Part: Young People and the Church	National Society/Church House Publishing
	TEACHING RESOURCES	
C16127Y	All Together Forever (Ephesians)	CPAS
C16129Y	Pressure Points (Issues)	CPAS
C16130Y	Harping On (Psalms)	CPAS
C16131Y	You'd Better Believe It! (Christian doctrine)	CPAS
C16132Y	Repeat Prescription (Ten Commandments)	CPAS
C16134Y	Powered Up (Acts)	CPAS
C16135Y	Just About Coping (Personal problems)	CPAS
C16136Y	Mission in Action (Mission)	CPAS
C16137Y	People With a Purpose (Bible characters)	CPAS
03604Y/		
03605Y	Whose Life Is It Anyway? (Christian Basics)	Andy Hickford, CPO
	Launchpad	Sue Clutterham, Scripture Union
	DRAMA RESOURCES	
C25121Y	Much Ado About Something	Andrew Smith, CPAS
C25122Y	Much Ado About Something Else	Andrew Smith, CPAS
	BIBLE COMMENTARIES	
	The Bible Speaks Today series	Various, IVP
	REFECTIVE, CREATIVE BIBLE APPROACH	
	Alive to God	Scripture Union
	Closer to God	Scripture Union
	PRACTICAL, HANDS-ON BIBLE APPROACH	
	Daily Bread	Scripture Union
	BIBLE STUDY NOTES	
	Encounter With God	Scripture Union
	BIBLE OVERVIEWS	
	According to Plan	Graeme Goldsworthy, Lancer/IVP
	Get Into the Bible	John Richardson, MPA Books
	WORSHIP RESOURCES	
C20010	DIY Worship	Simon Heathfield, CPAS
	MUSIC RESOURCES	
03123	Mission Praise Combined	MarshallPickering
	Let's Praise 1 and 2	MarshallPickering
	Wild Goose Songs Volumes 1-4	Wild Goose Publishing
		Spring Harvest Song Books Spring Harvest

The resources with a CPAS code are available from CPAS Sales on 01926 334242 during the day, or on 01926 335855 at any other time.